UNDERWATER RAID ON
Tirpitz

UNDERWATER RAID ON

Tirpitz

PETER HOWARD

Ian Allan
PUBLISHING

Acknowledgements:
The author wishes to thank the following:
Cdr J.J.Tall, RN, Director of the Royal Navy Submarine Museum at Gosport and his staff - in particular archivist George Malcolmson. Debbie Corner also at the Submarine Museum assisted with provision of photographs.
Elizabeth Selby at the Imperial War Museum, London.
The staff of the Royal Engineers Museum, Chatham.
Graham Thompson at the National Maritime Museum, Greenwich.
Tony Salter-Ellis at BAe Systems (Marine) Limited, Barrow-in-Furness.
Sabine Skae at The Dock Museum, Barrow-in-Furness.
Three survivors of X-craft trials and tribulations played a part: Robert Aitken, DSO; John Lorimer, DSO and Vernon Coles, DSM.
John Asmussen - for original images of *Tirpitz*.
Keith Faulkner - friend and long-serving former Royal Navy weapons specialist. Michael J. Gething - another friend, author and aviation specialist.

Further reading:
Benson, J. and Warren, C.E.T. *Above Us the Waves.*The Story of Midget Submarines and Human Torpedoes. (Harrap, 1953)
Broadhurst, R. *Churchill's Anchor: The Biography of Admiral of the Fleet Sir Dudley Pound* (Leo Cooper, 2000)
Churchill, W.S. *The Second World War, Vol 5. Closing the Ring* (Folio Society, 2000)
Compton-Hall, R. *Submarine Warfare: Monsters & Midgets* (Blandford Press, 1985)
Doenitz, K. *Memoirs: Ten Years and Twenty Days* (Cassell, 2000)
Harvey, D. *Monuments to Courage: Victoria Cross Headstones & Memorials Vol.2* (K & D. Patience, 1999)
Kemp, P. *Underwater Warriors: the Fighting History of Midget Submarines* (Cassell, 2000))
Kennedy, L. *Menace: the Life and Death of the Tirpitz* (Sidgwick & Jackson, 1979)
McMurtrie, F.E. (Ed.) *Jane's Fighting Ships 1942* (Sampson, Low, Marston & Co. 1943)
Sainsbury, A.B. *The Royal Navy Day by Day 2nd Edn.* (Ian Allan, 1992)
Walker, F. & Mellor,P. *The Mystery of X5: Lieutenant H. Henty Creer's attack on the Tirpitz* (William Kimber,1988)
Wheal, E-A. & Pope, S. (Eds.) *Macmillan Dictionary of The Second World War, 2nd Edn.* (Macmillan, 1997)

Series Created & Edited by Jasper Spencer-Smith.
Design and artwork: Nigel Pell.
Produced by JSS Publishing Limited,
PO. Box 6031, Bournemouth, Dorset, England.

First published 2006

ISBN (10)0 7110 3093 6
ISBN (13) 978 0 7110 3093 0

Published by Ian Allan Publishing

an imprint of Ian Allan Publishing Ltd, Hersham, Surrey KT12 4RG.
Printed by Ian Allan Printing Ltd, Hersham, Surrey KT12 4RG.

Code: 0604/C

Photograph Credits
John Asmussen (JA), British Aerospace (BAe),
The Dock Museum, Barrow-in-Furness (BM),
Imperial War Museum (IWM),
National Maritime Museum (NMM),
Royal Navy Submarine Museum (RNSM),
US Navy (USN).

CONTENTS

Tirpitz, when built, was the second largest ship in the German Navy. This 43,000-ton giant was commissioned in 1941 and was frequently referred to as 'The Beast' by Winston Churchill.

THE TARGET

Few single enemy units of warfare seemed to attract the attention of Winston Churchill in World War Two more than the *Tirpitz*, especially when the German Navy's second largest warship was moved to Norway in January 1942. Sister ship *Bismarck* had already had mixed fortunes in destroying the pride of the Royal Navy, HMS *Hood*, before being disabled, then destroyed, by a combination of British air and surface warfare skills.

Tirpitz displaced nearly 43,000 tons, had a top speed of 29 knots and mounted eight x 15-inch and 12 x 5.9-inch guns. Other armament included 102 anti-aircraft guns - 16 x 4.1-inch; 16 x 37mm; 70 x 20mm. The battleship also carried four Arado Ar196 aircraft and two catapults. Laid down at Wilhelmshaven in 1936, she was completed in 1941.

Britain's First Sea Lord and Chief of Naval Staff, Admiral of the Fleet Sir Dudley Pound, and his senior officers understood the threat posed by the *Tirpitz* to convoys heading for northern Russia - and Churchill sympathised with the predicament faced by the Royal Navy's over-stretched Home Fleet. Prime Minister

Left: **It is worth noting that the tops of the gun turrets and gun barrels are painted in a dark colour - the first signs of camouflage.** *Tirpitz* **at anchor in Brunsbüttel roads.** *(JA)*

Right: **The keel of *Tirpitz* is laid on 2 November 1936 on slipway No. 2 at the Kriegsmarine Werft in Wilhelms-haven, the vessel was given the construction No. S128. Here the hull frames are taking shape.** *(JA)*

Far right: **The launching of *Tirpitz* on 1 April 1939. The vessel was christened by Frau von Hassell, the daughter of Grand Admiral Tirpitz.** *(JA)*

Churchill persuaded President Franklin Delano Roosevelt to direct the United States Navy to assist in March 1942. Despite the damage inflicted on the US Navy at Pearl Harbor a few months earlier, and concerns over the situation in the Pacific Ocean, the Americans responded by sending the aircraft carrier USS *Wasp*, battleships USS *Washington* and USS *North Carolina* as well as two heavy cruisers and a destroyer squadron. This fleet, and the Home Fleet, had hoped to encounter *Tirpitz*, but it was not to be. Pound was the man who had instructed the convoy PQ17 to scatter in July 1942 in the belief the powerful German warship was steaming to attack the convoy - and 23 merchant ships and rescue boats were sunk by German submarines and the Luftwaffe.

When sheltering in the fjords, it was thought that *Tirpitz* was virtually impossible to attack from the air - and with coastal defences, virtually safe from surface raiders. While seaworthy she was a constant threat to Allied naval forces and merchant shipping moving to and from northern Russia. Something, clearly, had to be done ...but what?

Right: Tirpitz **under construction in the fitting out berth, 2 February 1940. The bridge structure is complete and the tower for observation and gunnery range finding is in place.** *(USN)*

Right: Tirpitz , for a warship, was a clean-lined ship. The hull was designed with a fine-shaped bow and a clean rounded stern. The photograph shows the ship being assisted whilst manoeuvring in Kaafjord, Norway. *(USN)*

Left: The *Tirpitz* berthed at the entrance to the Inner Dockyard Basin in Kiel Harbour, September 1941. *(IWM)*

Below: The newly completed *Tirpitz* leaves the fitting-out dock and basin at Wilhelmshaven. The vessel is not under its own power so it is being towed and positioned by dockyard tugs. *(JA)*

On 5 May 1941
Adolf Hitler
visited the
Gotenhafen
dockyard to
inspect *Tirpitz*.
(AN)

Left: **Crew members muster under the aft main armament. Note the framework floats which were used to carry foliage as camouflage.** *(USN)*

Left: **Canvas covers were fitted over the main armament to 'disguise' *Tirpitz* from aerial reconnaissance aircraft. Barges with wooden frameworks covered in foliage were positioned around the ship to further disguise its shape.** *(USN)*

Right: **The crew muster for light entertainment, whilst two young ladies 'strut their stuff' on the afterdeck of *Tirpitz* when moored in Fæhenfjord, near Trondheimfjord, Norway, 1942. (USN)**

Right: **Obscured with canvas covers, foliage and camouflage barges, *Tirpitz* 'hides' in Fæhenfjord, Norway, 1942. (USN)**

Many attempts were made to design and produce a midget submarine. The first instance of a vessel being used for an underwater attack was in 1776 against HMS Eagle.

2

THE MEANS AND THE MEN

The idea of a midget submarine was not new. Indeed, earlier in the war the Japanese and the Italians had achieved some success with small underwater craft. The Italians attacked the Royal Navy battleships HMS *Queen Elizabeth* and HMS *Valiant* in Alexandria harbour using a piloted torpedo device (*Maiale* - [Pig]) in December 1941 - and earlier in that month five Japanese two-man craft (A-type) had taken part in the attack on Pearl Harbor. The small submarines were not very successful and one was captured by US forces after running aground. The other four were sunk. Japanese midget submarines were also used for an attack in Sydney Harbour. A further attack resulted in damage to the battleship HMS *Ramillies*, at Madagascar, in 1942. Germany did not achieve much with similar underwater activities.

The concept of small submarines can be traced back to Alexander the Great, with infrequent attempts to test the theory afterwards. One famous instance was the unsuccessful attack by the Americans using *Turtle* on HMS *Eagle* in New York harbour in

Left: **A captured Japanese navy A-type midget submarine. This two-man craft was first used in the attack on Pearl Harbor, 7 December 1941.** *(RNSM)*

Far left: The Turtle **a semi-submersible used in an unsuccessful underwater attack on HMS *Eagle* when the ship was at anchor in New York Harbour, 1776.** *(RNSM)*

Right: **His Majesty's Torpedo Boat No. 1 (*Holland 1*) underway off Gosport (Portsmouth). At the helm is the Coxswain, Petty Officer Waller. *Holland 1* was launched on 2 October 1901 at the yard of Vickers Son & Maxim Limited in Barrow-in-Furness, Cumbria, north-east England. (RNSM)**

September 1776. *Turtle*, mainly constructed from wood and shaped like a World War Two British-type hand grenade was technically a semi-submersible but many historians regard this assault on Lord Howes' 64-gun flagship as the first evidence of an attack by submarine. In the 19th century, advances in technology and weaponry led to several nations attempting to develop submarine torpedo boats - shortened later to the now familiar submarine. American Robert Fulton was a painter and inventor who went to Paris in 1797 and in 1801 tested a five-man

submarine at Camaret sur Mer, near Brest, France. Neither French nor British governments were interested. The early 20th century was the setting for the launch of the Royal Navy's first submarine, *Holland 1* on 2 October 1901, at Barrow-in-Furness, Cumbria in north-west England. Designed by Irish-American John Philip Holland and without a name at birth, she became just HM s/mn No.1. Holland died in 1914 - when experts were studying with interest drawings of two- and three-man submarines produced by Robert H. Davis

Right: **The *Maiale* (Pig) was developed by the Italian Navy as a piloted torpedo. It was used in an attack in December 1941 against the battleships HMS *Queen Elizabeth* and HMS *Valiant* in Alexandria Harbour, Egypt. (RNSM)**

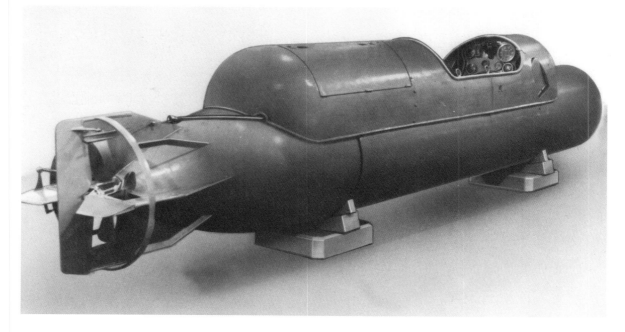

Left: **A British two-man 'Human Torpedo' (known as the Chariot, and crew as Charioteers) without the detachable explosive charge which fitted on the front of the machine. The Chariot was used in Operation 'Title', an aborted raid on** *Tirpitz* **in October 1942.** *(RNSM)*

Centre: **A Chariot Mk II on a training exercise in Loch Cairnbawn, Scotland. In the background is the depot ship HMS** *Bonaventure.* *(RNSM)*

Below: **The 'Human Torpedo' (Chariot) was first used in a night attack on the Italian naval base of Palermo, northern Sicily, 3 January 1943. The warship** *Ulpio Traiano* **was sunk and the transport** *Viminale* **badly damaged.** *(RNSM)*

Above: **Royal Navy divers undergoing endurance training on a rudimentary exercise bicycle.** *(RNSM)*

Above right: **His Majesty King George VI inspecting Charioteers on the deck of HMS *Bonaventure*.** *(RNSM)*

Right: **The diving suit for Charioteers was of the 'dry' type; sealed at the neck, wrists and ankles. Note the air bottles carried at the back of the waist.** *(RNSM)*

in his manual *Deep Diving and Submarine Operations*.

This two-part manual for deep sea divers and compressed air workers reached an 8th edition in 1981, published by Siebe Gorman & Company Limited - for whom Davis was variously director, managing director and chairman. The 1914 drawings incorporated one of his creations - for which submariners were to be particularly grateful - the Davis Submarine Escape Apparatus (DSEA).

Even before World War One, Commander (Cdr.) Godfrey Herbert, DSO, RN, had projected his 'Devastator', which could be described as a cross between a human torpedo and a midget submarine. This invention did have a design for allowing the human to leave the vessel at some point before the torpedo sped on to the target! Cdr. Herbert sold his idea to Vickers Armstrong Limited.

Returning to World War Two and the problem of the *Tirpitz*, the German Navy had troubles of its own with mine damage to *Scharnhorst* and *Gneisenau* whilst *Prinz Eugen* had suffered damage by a British torpedo. All three ships should have joined *Tirpitz*, *Admiral Scheer* and *Hipper* in Norwegian waters and although the naval force 'at Trondheim was only half as strong as Hitler had hoped, it riveted our attention', Churchill wrote in his six-volume book '*The Second World War*'. He frequently referred to the *Tirpitz* as 'The Beast'.

Left: **An early version of the Davis Submarine Escape Equipment (DESA). Only minor modifications were made before it was issued to the Royal Navy Submarine Service.** *(RNSM)*

Between the two world wars, the Royal Navy had not seen much future in midget submarines, and if their Lordships of the Admiralty had thought about them in the late 1930s, they clearly felt that countering the threat posed by the new German capital ships to their own major surface ships was a much bigger priority. When the Navy tried to attack *Tirpitz* using chariots (two-man torpedo) the raid was a failure caused by bad weather. One naval historian, Dr Eric Grove, claimed the idea of building midget submarines for the purpose of attacking

Left: **A crewman exits an escape hatch on a submarine during an exercise. The DESA has not been inflated.** *(RNSM)*

Right: **A shipbuilder's model of the first production X-craft which was to be built by Vickers-Armstrong Limited at the company's Barrow-in-Furness yard.** *(BM)*

German warships in Norway (largely immune to bombing or surface attack) is to the credit of retired submariner, Cdr. Cromwell H. Varley, DSC, RN. Another naval specialist, author Paul Kemp believed that a British Army officer named Jefferis should get the credit.

Major (Maj.) Millis Rowland Jefferis, a Royal Engineer, was a General Staff Officer, second grade (GSO2) in 1939 on the staff of Chief of the Imperial General Staff, General Sir Edmund Ironside, GCB, CMG, DSO. Jefferis, who won the Military Cross (MC) in Waziristan (North West Frontier territory now in Pakistan) in the early 1920s, became a war service lieutenant-colonel and temporary brigadier in one day in 1942! The War Office offered the services of Jefferis to the Navy once the Admiralty had agreed to take over design and production of a midget submarine (originally destined for river or harbour use by the Army) at a meeting of Controller of the Navy in July 1940. Jefferis (who later spent most of the war in the Ministry of Supply concentrating on the development of special weapons) was to assist in the production of a staff requirement as the Controller of the Navy

Right: **A port-side view of the same model which is displayed as part of the Vickers-Armstrong collection at The Dock Museum, Barrow-in-Furness.** *(BM)*

Left: X3 inside the catamaran shelter designed to hide the midget submarine whilst being towed out to sea for trials. *(NMM)*

Below left: **The X-craft prototype being carefully reversed out of the catamaran.** *(IWM)*

Below: **His Majesty's Drifter** *Present Help*, **commanded by Lt. 'George' Washington RN, with the protective catamaran alongside.** *(IWM)*

Above: **Major Millis Rowland Jefferis of the Royal Engineers in the main hatch of *X3*. Note the hatch for the Wet & Dry (W&D) compartment at the front of the superstructure. *X3* was launched in great secrecy after dark at 23.00 on Sunday 15 March 1942.** *(IWM)*

and his staff took over the project. Cdr. 'Crom' Varley had established Varley-Marine Works Limited at Sarisbury Green on the Hamble river near Southampton and with Cdr. T.I.S. Bell, RN, under the supervision of Director of Naval Construction (DNC), pressed ahead with *X3* and *X4*, the prototypes for the X-craft. Cromwell Varley, a descendant of the Lord Protector, Oliver Cromwell, was an experienced submariner and as a lieutenant with the 8th Flotilla based at the port of Great Yarmouth, Norfolk on the east coast of England, was commanding HM s/mn *H5* when the German submarine *U15* was torpedoed and sunk on the 14 July 1916 near the Ems estuary in northern Germany. Also commanding a submarine based with the 8th Flotilla was Lieutenant-Commander (Lt.-Cdr.) Godfrey Herbert, DSO, RN, mentioned earlier. Varley died in 1949 aged 59 and a *Times* obituary said of him: 'Crom' Varley was a typical naval officer of the best type, and readily identified as such without the aid of uniform, by his breeziness, geniality and good natured consideration for others'. The obituary said he had a great deal of the forthrightness of his ancestor - 'while

he conspicuously lacked the less attractive characteristics of that great man'.

Construction of the midget submarine prototypes was not possible in naval dockyards because these were stretched to the limit with building new surface ships - or refits and repairs to war damaged vessels. Varley was to be responsible for the design and production of the prototypes and the DNC would assist - while examining the design with future requirements in mind. It is surprising in the early years of the 21st century when there is so much criticism of the length of time it takes in peacetime to bring new equipment into being, to look back and consider how much was achieved speedily in wartime. Think of the Mark I tank in World War One; and of the Barnes Wallis-designed 'bouncing bomb' of 'Dambusters' fame. X-craft deserve to feature in such achievements. Bearing in mind the need to design, build and test the prototypes the Admiralty did not take control of what became the 'X-craft project' until April 1940. The first of the operational craft (*X5* to *X10*) were laid down at the Barrow-in-Furness shipyard of Vickers-Armstrong Limited in September 1942. The first of the class was

Left: **X3** **on sea trials in the Solent off Portsmouth. Trials were also carried out with mock attacks against Portland Harbour, Weymouth Bay, Dorset. The crew for the trials was Lt. W. G. Meeke, DSC, RN (commanding officer), Lt. D. Cameron, RNR (1st Lieutenant) and Chief ERA Richardson. Cameron was to command** *X6* **on the** *Tirpitz* **raid.** *(IWM)*

Left: **Going astern. Note how the stern of** *X3* **is underwater due to the pull of the propeller.** *(IWM)*

Left: **Commander Cromwell Varley in the main hatch of** *X3.* **Note the Barr & Stroud periscope is mounted in the W&D hatch. This was moved on production X-craft.** *(IWM)*

Right: X3 at sea on main engine trials. A shelter (dodger) has been fitted around the main hatch to prevent swamping. Also the engine room intake mast is erected. HM Drifter *Present Help* and catamaran are at top right. *(IWM)*

Below: Major Jefferis in *X3*. The hawse pipe for the tow was modified on production craft to allow a flat foredeck. *(IWM)*

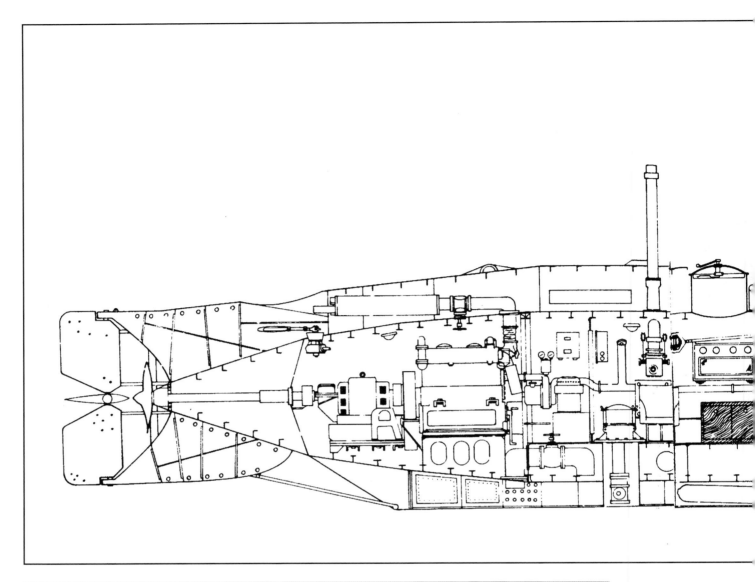

Above: **A schematic drawing of a production X-craft.**

Left: **The only bunk for resting was situated in the bow of the X-craft over the battery compartment. If sleep was possible another hazard was fumes from the batteries causing headaches or nausea to crew members.** *(RNSM)*

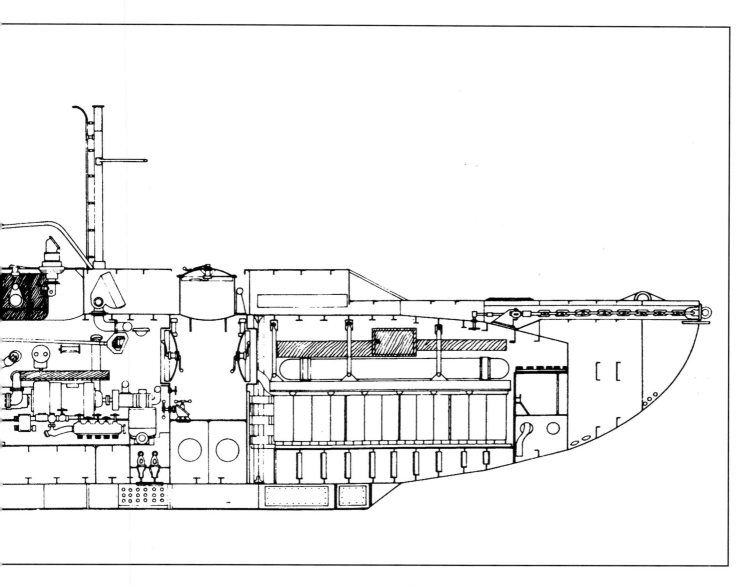

delivered at the end of December that year and the sixth (*X10*) and last on 8 February 1943.

The midget submarine designed in the experienced submariner hands of the enthusiastic Varley was to have many changes from the British Army's Jefferis-designed craft (submersible and suitable for rivers or harbours) in order for it to be effective for service at sea. Because of the need for secrecy in approaching the German warship hideouts in the fjords, and the need for something more reliable than the chariot method, the submarine had to be the best method of delivery. The X-craft did not carry torpedoes, but charges port and starboard on the sides of the hull to be released under, or as near as possible to, the hull of the target. These charges – or mines – released from controls inside the X-craft would each weigh 4 tons (4,064kg), contain 2 tons (2,032kg) of Amatex explosive

and be detonated by clock time fuses. Amatex is a highly sensitive military chemical explosive containing 40% RDX, 40% TNT and 20% ammonium nitrate. The charges had three divisions, the centre one contained the explosive.

An essential element of the X-craft design was a compartment known as 'Wet &Dry' (W&D) from which a diver could exit and enter through a hatch in the deck when the vessel was submerged. The diver equipped with DSEA flooded the compartment to exit, and, on return after net-cutting, laying charges or any other task, could re-enter via the hatch and pump out the water. Special diving suits were to be provided for this purpose and survivor Robert Aitken, of whom more later, recalled what the diver had to do: 'This meant getting into a diving suit, climbing into and flooding the W&D (which could be done by

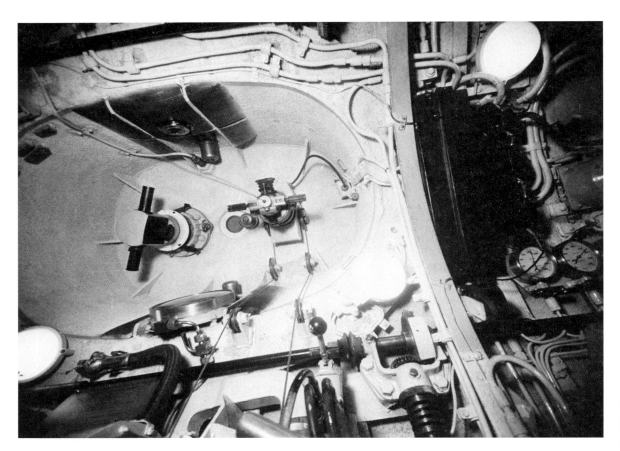

Left: **The Barr & Stroud miniature periscope mounted ahead of the direction finder in the superstructure for use by the Commanding Officer.** *(BAe)*

Right: **A view taken from the W&D compartment. To the left is the helmsman's seat, in the centre is the periscope and at the rear the diesel engine.** *(BAe)*

pumping water from one of the other tanks to avoid altering the buoyancy), waiting for the pressure to equalise before opening the hatch and climbing out and onto the casing. Then the cutter, which was connected to an airline hose, had to be taken from a locker in the casing, hooked onto a wire of the net, the valve opened and the first wire was cut. That was straightforward, as long as the bow was pushing into the net and the boat was at a right angle to the net. If the boat was alongside the net, which happened occasionally, a larger hole usually had to be cut and the boat manoeuvred through. This took much longer and was exhausting'. The W&D could also be used for escape in emergency. The craft had an induction mast - with safety rail - down which orders could be related to the man at the helm, and a Barr & Stroud miniature periscope. This later revealed operating problems, particularly where *X6* and *X10* were concerned.

Varley-Marine Works Limited pressed on with the design of the prototypes *X3* and *X4* and assembled *X3* at Sarisbury Green, with *X4* being completed by HM Dockyard, Portsmouth. Though there were some minor differences between the two prototypes, at 45ft (13.72m) *X4* was slightly longer than the 43ft 6in (13.26m) of *X3*.

Most of the specifications were common:
Beam: 5ft 6in (1.68m)
Draught (forward): 5ft 1in (1.55m)
(aft) 7ft (2.13m)
Displacement (surfaced): 22 tons (22,352.9kg) (*X4* 23 tons [23,368.96kg])
(dived): 24 tons (24,385kg) (*X4* 25 tons [25,401kg])
Endurance (surfaced): 1,400 nautical miles at 4.5 kts
(dived): 85 nautical miles at 2 kts
Speed (surfaced): 6 kts - cruising 4.5 kts
(dived): max 5 kts - cruising 2 kts
Diving depth (operational): 200ft (60.96m)
Engine: one Gardner 32 four-cylinder water-cooled diesel
Engine (dived): Keith Blackman 32hp electric

The pressure hull was circular and made of 8lb (3.63kg) steel plating with 1.5in (38mm) x 1.5in (38mm) x 1.79lb (.81kg) angle bars every 6.5in (165mm). It was built in three sections and constructed by three different companies:

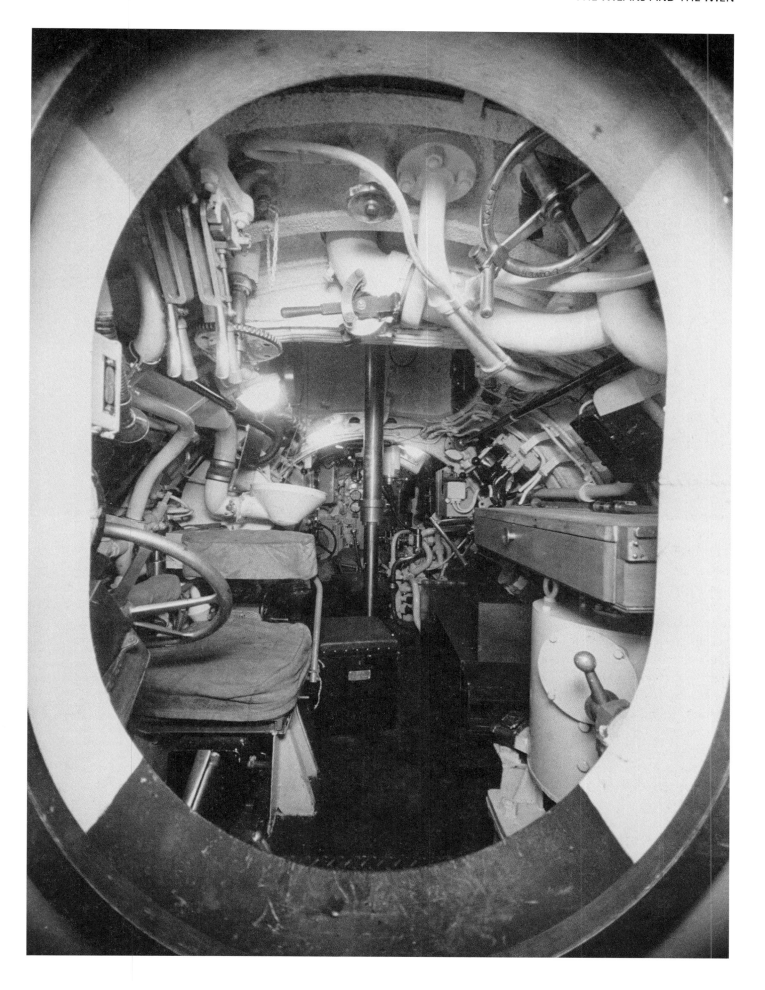

Thornycroft (fore), Vickers-Armstrong (mid) and Brigham & Cowan (aft), all three companies acting on behalf of Varley-Marine. Late at night on 15 March 1942, *X3* was launched with the first dive taking place in the Solent towards the end of that month. The vessel having made a promising debut was taken to Southampton Docks in August. From here a train took the still very secret *X3* to Faslane in Scotland. While the trials were proceeding, DNC was considering what to do next, in the event that they proved successful. Vickers-Armstrong was asked to take on the design of follow-on craft and among changes Admiral (Submarines) wanted incorporated were:

A pressure hull to withstand a depth of 300ft (91.44m)

Surface endurance reduced to 1200 nautical miles at 4kts

Submerged endurance – (without recharging) 80 nautical miles at 2kts. *X5* to *X10* carried Exide 20 SP batteries.

The operational X-craft were all fitted with a Gardner 42 four-cylinder water-cooled diesel engine and Keith Blackman main (electric) motor generating 30hp at 1,650rpm – 2hp less than in the prototypes.

Navigation in the operational craft was by a Browns A-type gyrocompass and though *X3* did not have a direction indicator, *X4* was fitted with an AFV 6A/602 - and this Air Ministry model was also fitted in the operational craft. Navigation was carried out mainly by the commanding officer (CO).

Hydrophones were first fitted to midget submarines as a safety measure, designed to assist in avoiding other vessels during training exercises. After numerous experiments a Type 151 target indicator was used in the six operational X-craft. The equipment, comprising transmitter, receiver, cathode ray tube and other essentials weighed just 53lb (24kg) - an ingenious piece of scaling down. With all this miniaturisation, the X-craft could achieve manoeuvres beyond the capability of

Above: **The handle at the centre is to control the trim of the X-craft.** *(BAe)*

Right: **Construction of X-51 HMS/m *Stickleback*, the last X-craft, was carried out by Vickers-Armstrong Limited at Barrow-in-Furness. This sequence of photographs is dated 16 May 1954.** *(BAe)*

the large submarines in that X-craft could hover and change depth vertically. However, nothing could change the fact that the 51ft (15.55m) long X-craft, of which everything internally had to fit into around 35ft (10.67m), meant for uncomfortable living for the crews. In the forward compartment there was one bunk above the batteries. Sleep was not easy and because of the position of the bunk, could mean waking up with a headache caused by battery fumes.

The passage crew of three had to have food and water for 10 days as they faced an eight-day tow to the target area in Norway before handing over to the operational crew. As mentioned, the captain did the navigating, his number one (or 'Jimmy' - the first lieutenant) took care of the helm, propulsion, trimming and hydroplane controls, relieved when necessary by the engine room artificer (ERA)… when he was not looking after equipment!

The operational crew, carried in the towing submarine, would be transferred by dinghy before the attack. For this the crew was

Left: **The first production X-craft *X5* in a workshop at Vickers-Armstrong Limited. Note the flush foredeck and the position of the hawse pipe for the towing rope/cable. The Barr & Stroud periscope is in the full-extended position. The engine air-intake pipe is in the 'surfaced' position.** *(RNSM)*

Above: **A starboard view of *X5* showing the clean 'lines' of the vessel. The external explosive side charges were mounted around the ballast tank on each side. The hatch to the W&D compartment is open and the engine air-intake pipe is erected.** *(RNSM)*

Left: **The stern of *X5* showing the mountings and controls for the rudders and hydroplanes.** *(RNSM)*

increased to four by the inclusion of a diver for the attack. The passage crews were returned to the towing submarine.

One of the most important design improvements involved moving the W&D compartment from amidships to forward of the control room. Veterans remember that moving around was awkward enough when the W&D was in dry mode. When it was flooded, then movement was out of the question. Neither *X3* nor *X4* were used in operations but had a significant part to play in the testing of equipment and the training of crews.

The official Royal Navy Battle Summary No. 29 published in 1945 as a 'Confidential' document gave brief details of the X-craft:

Length: 51ft (15.55m)
Beam: 8ft 6in (2.59m)
Overall height: 10ft (3.05m)
Surface draught: 7ft 6in (2.29m)
Weight: 35 ton (35,561.47kg)
Diving depth: 300ft (91.44m)
Maximum surface speed on main engines: 6.5kts

Range (limited by human endurance): 1,500 nautical miles at 4kts
Maximum submerged speed on main motors: 5kts
Submerged endurance - (without recharging batteries): 80 nautical miles at 2kts
Crew endurance: 10-14 days
Armament: Two detachable side charges, each containing 2 tons (2,032kg) of Amatex, dropped on the seabed under the target, and detonated by clock timer fuses
Crew: (operational) - three officers (including one qualified diver), one Engine Room Artificer (ERA) (passage) – one officer, one able seaman LTO (Leading Torpedo Man), one stoker.

Cdr. Richard Compton-Hall RN, given command of an X-craft after the war and for many years Director of the Royal Navy Submarine Museum at Gosport, Hampshire, described how one looked: 'The whole thing, out of the water, resembled an old-fashioned railway boiler. In fact, being appointed to command a midget was rather like being given

Left: **A later X-craft being hoisted aboard HMS *Bonaventure* with side-charges mounted. Note the completely flat keel to allow the vessel to safely 'ground' on the seabed.** *(RNSM)*

Right: **The view aft towards the engine room shows how cramped the conditions were on board an X-craft.** *(RNSM)*

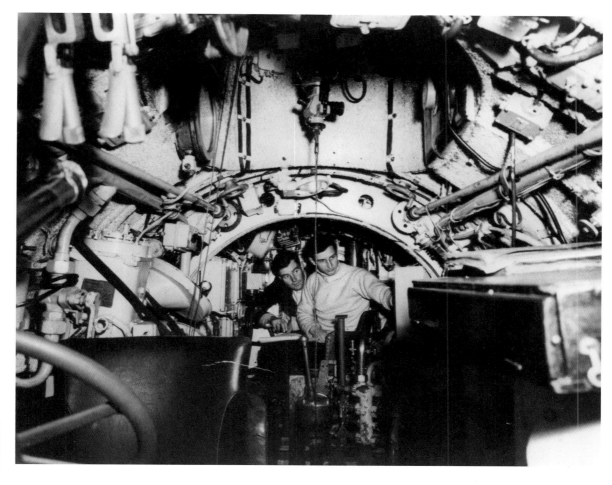

a toy train set for Christmas. It was a perfect submarine in miniature. Everything was scaled down …main-vent hand levers, valve wheels, high-pressure air bottles, battery cells, gauges, indicators and the main periscope, which itself was a masterpiece of miniaturization, but delicate and prone to faults. The 42-horsepower diesel engine that drove the craft on the surface and recharged the battery was the same as that fitted to a London omnibus - it proved just as trustworthy rumbling throatily up the Norwegian fjords as on the streets of the metropolis. Simplicity and ruggedness were the key words in design and construction. In the main X-craft were robust and reliable. They could - and did - thump the bottom and run full tilt, if inadvertently, into solid obstructions without harm. The safe diving depth was 300 feet (91.44m) (with a 75% safety factor below that), and resistance to depth-charge shockwaves was comparable with normal submarines'.

With the six Vickers-Armstrong-built X-craft handed over by February 1943, there were some senior officers who hoped they could be used on operations that spring, before Norwegian daylight hours became too long. The 9 March date had been selected as a last chance for that season - but this did not allow sufficient time for training to be completed.

On 17 April 1943, as Battle Summary No. 29 records, the 12th Submarine Flotilla was formed under Captain W. (Willy) E. Banks, DSC, RN. HMS *Varbel* at Port Bannatyne on the Isle of Bute in the west of Scotland was the base - named after the X-craft prototype designers *Var*ley and *Bel*l . The flotilla's role was to co-ordinate, 'the training and materiel of the special weapons'. To this flotilla *X5* to *X10* were attached, with HMS *Bonaventure* (Acting Captain P. Q. Roberts, RN) as depot ship.

HMS *Bonaventure* was being built at Greenock for the Clan Line as a Cameron class steamer when she was commandeered by the Royal Navy. The ship was equipped to lift the midget submarines on board for servicing. HMS *Bonaventure* should not be confused with the Dido-class cruiser of the same name, torpedoed by a U-boat while on convoy duty in April 1941.

Left: **Port Bannatyne, The Isle of Bute, in the west of Scotland. Named HMS *Varbel* after the X-craft designers *Var* (Varley) and *bel* (Bell) it was the headquarters for the 12th Submarine Flotilla under the command of Captain W.E. Banks, DSC, RN from 17 April 1943.** *(RNSM)*

Left: **Fort Blockhouse (HMS *Dolphin*) the home of the Royal Navy's submarine forces, photographed in the autumn of 1945.** *(RNSM)*

Above: **HMS Bonaventure, the depot ship for X-craft. The ship was originally built for the Clan shipping line as a Cameron class steamer. In 1948 she was returned to the British Merchant Navy as *Clan Davidson 2* until being scrapped at Hong Kong in 1961.** (RNSM)

Right: **XE-craft on the deck of HMS Bonaventure, in service during 1945 in the Pacific. Note that on two of the vessels the cover plates on the side charges have been removed, allowing the explosive mixture to be unloaded. The craft on the left is a limpet mine carrier.** (RNSM)

Above: **Passage and Operational crews for Operation 'Source', the raid on *Tirpitz*, assembled on the deck of HMS *Bonaventure*.** *(RNSM)*

Left: **The Commanding Officer of HMS *Bonaventure*, Captain W.R. Fell (right) with Lt. Cdr. J.F.B. Brown stand by the nameplate, crest and ship's bell.** *(RNSM)*

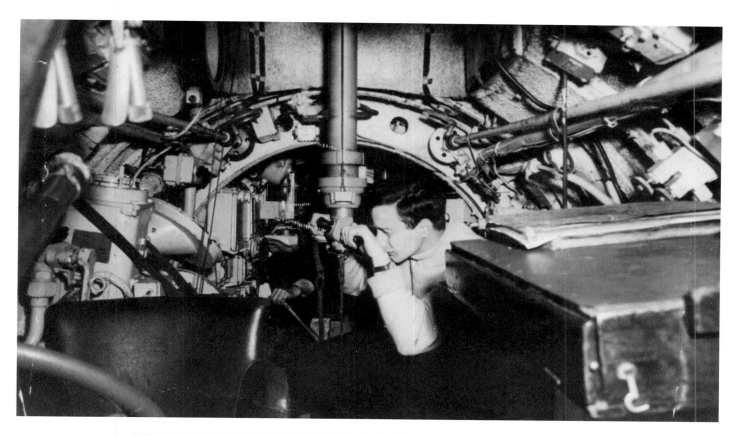

Above: **Lt. Verry at the Barr & Stroud miniature periscope inside an early (probably** *X5* **to** *X10***) X-craft.** *(RNSM)*

Right: **Number One (1st Lieutenant) Sub Lt. 'Robbie' Robinson, RNVR at the trimming controls of an X-craft. The carpenter's glue pot at the lower edge of this photograph was used to produce the only hot food to be eaten on board. It is worth comparing these photographs with those of the interior of the later craft** *X51* **on pages 24 to 28.** *(RNSM)*

Left: X20 was used for Operation 'Postage Able' (reconnaissance of the Normandy beaches) and Operation 'Gambit' (marking the landing areas on D-Day) 6 June 1944. The vessel was commanded by Lt. Hudspeth, RANVR. *(NMM)*

Below: X23 was used with *X20* to mark landing beaches on 6 June 1944 as part of Operation 'Gambit' under the command of Lt. J. Honour, RNVR. *X23* was sold with *X20* for scrap in 1945. *(NMM)*

HMS *Bonaventure* was used later in the Pacific with XE-craft and after Japan surrendered became a naval transport steaming to and from Australia, Japan, China, Malaya and the Philippines. In 1948 the ship was back in British Merchant Navy service as *Clan Davidson 2* until scrapped in Hong Kong in 1961.

The limiting factor of the X-craft was the endurance of the crews, and for this reason each submarine had two crews: one for the passage and one for the attack. The battle summary mentions intensive training being carried out in the summer of 1943 at Loch Cairnbawn (Loché Cháirn Báhn) at the head of Eddrachillis Bay (northwest coast of Scotland), under Cdr. D. C. Ingram, DSC, RN. Training included realistic exercises against capital ships of the Home Fleet defended by anti-torpedo nets and equipment specially

Right: **His Majesty's Submarine *X25* under power of the diesel engine. Note the positions of the W&D hatch and main hatch.** *(IWM)*

Below: X25 **photographed in April 1944. As on earlier X-craft the foredeck is clear of obstructing equipment allowing safe movement for the crew. The vessel is not carrying side charges. *X25* which was built in 1944 by Marshall's of Gainsborough and later sold for scrap in 1945.** *(IWM)*

supplied by the Boom Defence Organisation.

Robert Aitken, who had probably the most traumatic operational experience in managing to escape from the sunken *X7*, had not long left school and interrupted his articles for accountancy when he volunteered for naval service. He trained as a charioteer before 'volunteering' for midget submarines. Talking to the author in March 2005 he said that the training was 'tremendous fun' and interviewed for the *Lost Heroes* programme, he recalled: 'When I joined the Navy, and still in civilian clothes, I had a medical examination and was told to report to my divisional officer, who told me I had defective colour vision and asked if I wanted to be a stoker or a steward. I said if I was not wanted as a seaman I'd try the Army. My divisional officer decided the best thing would be to allow me to complete my preliminary training as a seaman. In due

Left: **The engine room intake mast also carried a map reading light and voice pipe for the commanding officer. To the right, protected by 'crash bars', is the optical head of the Barr & Stroud periscope.** *(IWM)*

course I'd find myself at sea and would then have to say that I had defective colour vision. When I eventually did so, the Officer of the Watch simply said, 'Nonsense, you wouldn't be here if you were'.

I was able to complete the minimum three months at sea before going on to officers' training. After that I had a humdrum job because no one knew what to do with a colour-blind midshipman, until one day the appointments officer said: 'There's a job which might accept two colour-blind people. Are you interested?' Keen to get away from the humdrum job, it was not until he arrived at

HMS *Dolphin* in Gosport, the main base of the submarine service, that he realised he was not going to have anything to do with submarines. Aitken continues, 'You did as you were told in the Navy, but at age 19 and having been well disciplined at school, I didn't find that difficult. As far as we all were concerned it was a marvellous summer on the west coast of Scotland. We were kept active, our days were roughly divided into three periods of eight hours each - training, keeping fit and sleeping. What better part of the world to do those three things? Also, if you give a teenager what is essentially an underwater motorbike that's

Right: **The Commanding Officer (CO) of *X25*, Lt. Smart RN enters the vessel through the W&D hatch. Note the bar and safety strap for the CO mounted on the engine room intake mast. This was designed by Lt. A. R. Hezlet, DSC, RN (a highly respected submarine commander), the safety officer for the flotilla, and was known as the 'Hezlet rail'. The bar at the front of the superstructure is to prevent snagging when the vessel penetrates anti-submarine netting.** *(IWM)*

great fun. Between the training exercises we could chase crabs and other fish. Life was taken light-heartedly'. Robert Aitken and some fellow charioteers, when asked to transfer to X-craft, declined at first. The CO of the 12th Submarine Flotilla travelled from the Clyde, said he understood their reasons but wondered if they would go to the Clyde to see a mock-up of a W&D compartment. He also offered a few days leave in Glasgow - and so got the charioteers' help!

John Lorimer, the first lieutenant (number one) in *X6*, joined the Royal Navy in 1941 and was one of the 'originals' on X-craft. In his

transcript from the 2004 BBC programme for television he remembered training two volunteers in *X3* on 4 November 1942 when the craft sank, stern first, in about 120ft (36.6m) – 'and the water in the bilges entered the batteries and created chlorine gas, which is lethal. We decided we had to equalise the pressure inside and outside in order to escape. There's only one way to do that and that was to flood the craft. One of the people I was training became a bit excited, and the more excited he became the more he breathed oxygen. We had four Davis escape sets, and he finished his set and I managed to get the other set onto him.

Then the other trainee managed to get the hatch open and I pushed the first man through, but it was a close-run thing. Within twelve hours, a boom defence vessel came along and lifted *X3*, but I wasn't the most popular man because she was the prototype, and I'd been forced to sink her. She was taken to Faslane and put on low-loader train - *X3* was crated up by shipwrights in an enormous long wooden box - and I was detailed to escort her down to Portsmouth for repair. Four sailors joined me as guards. It took us eleven days to get from Faslane to Portsmouth, and we stopped at a siding in Glasgow, where I put two sailors on guard with their fixed bayonets. A small Glaswegian boy of about eight came up to look at us and said, 'What have you got there, mister? A wee submarine?' So much for security'.

Vernon 'Ginger' Coles, ERA 4 in *X9* was one of the men who trained hard for the attack on German warships in northern Norway. He was to be disappointed when, as part of the operational crew, the loss of *X9* en-route ended the operation for him and the other three crewmen. Coles joined the Royal Navy in 1938 and had seen action in the Leader-class destroyer HMS *Faulknor*, the flotilla leader involved in the sinking of the first U-boat in the war, *U39* and another, *U27*, five days later. He also had seen action off Narvik in Norway, in the Mediterranean and the attack on *Tirpitz'* sister ship, *Bismarck* before he attended an advance engineering course and then volunteered for submarines. Interviewed by the Newbury Probus Club, Coles said the most frightening thing about your first dive is 'not the claustrophobia or any submerged feeling but simply the ear shattering noises a 'sub' makes when blowing ballast'. In Scotland when training began in earnest for the X-craft, Coles - who was to become the longest serving member - recalled training 'to use specially designed diving suits using full oxygen and how to work underwater, cutting through links of heavy chain, using a hammer and cold chisel and the use of a flame cutter'.

Training, especially when using new equipment with which few people had experience, was never easy - and as happens with trials, it can be costly.

Sub-Lieutenant Ivor ('Taffy') Thomas, RNVR, was swept off the casing of *X4* and drowned in December 1942 and Sub-Lieutenant David H. Locke, RNVR, was lost from *X7* in a diving, net-cutting accident in Lock Striven, May 1943. His place was taken by Lieutenant (Lt.) L.B. (Bill) Whittam, RNVR - one of two men to die in *X7* during the attack on *Tirpitz*. 'Once we had confidence in the equipment we began to use it effectively,' Vernon Coles states. 'We had to go down and off the beach on a lifeline and we had to stay down as long as we possibly could under water, which was anything up to six hours, and then we were pulled out. You gave four tugs on your lifeline as a signal that you were in trouble. Edmund Goddard, who was the ERA of *X6*, was out there at the same time as me and he was running out of oxygen so he gave four tugs and the midshipman on the other end paid him out more line instead of pulling him up. Eddie then decided to keep pulling the line until the midshipman was left with the end in his hand, at which point he decided there must be something wrong down there. Eddie came out and he was black in the face and unconscious. The midshipman left the job that day and was sent back to general service. Some people were kicked out at that stage. They just couldn't take the training and the strain; we lost quite a few people like that - sent back to big submarines or general service'.

The Battle Summary recorded, 'Special security measures were instituted at Loch Cairnbarn (*sic*) and, after 1 September, were increased in stringency. No leave was given, none but specially selected officers and ratings were allowed to leave the area, and all ships were retained in the port till after the completion of the operation'. Cdr Ingram was later praised by Adm Barry, who said the commander 'by his leadership and ability as officer in charge of training, inspired all officers and ratings alike and achieved that high standard of training and fitness which was so essential. He was responsible that the crews were at the peak of their efficiency at the time the operation began'.

Right: **Detail of the engine room intake mast. Note the Barr & Stroud periscope in the fully-up position.** *(RNMS)*

Although it would have been possible for the X-craft independently to get to Norway under power, it was decided that towing was preferential to save the crews from severe fatigue.

3

THE PLAN - OPERATION 'SOURCE'

One of the biggest problems facing the planners was movement of the X-craft from their base in Scotland to Altenfjord (now Altafjord), a distance of over 1,000 miles (1,609.3km). Yes, the X-craft could get there under power. But what state would the crews be in before any attack? The craft could have been loaded onto a surface vessel with the right lifting capacity, but then there was the problem of being spotted from the sea or air en-route, with all the hazards that would involve. Eventually, towing by 'mother' submarines was the chosen option. As for timing and weather, the Battle Summary continues: 'Meanwhile detailed plans for the operation were being prepared by the Staff of the Rear-Admiral, Submarines. In order to complete the operation before winter weather conditions were likely to set in, it was decided that the attack should take place at the earliest date on which the hours of darkness permitted. A certain amount of moonlight was necessary to assist the X-craft in the navigation of the fjords, and as the period 20-25 September 1943, with the moon in the last quarter, fulfilled these conditions,

Left: **A rare photograph of an X-craft which was used in the attack on** *Tirpitz.* **On the deck of** *X10* **is Sub Lt. Page, one of the passage crew. Loch Cairnbawn (referred to as Cairnbarn in the Battle Summary) from where the midget submarines were towed for the attack is located at the head of Eddrachillis Bay on the north-east coast of Scotland.** *(RNSM)*

Right: **HMS/m *X24* at her moorings at Balta Sound on Unst, the most northerly of the Shetland Islands. The vessel is flying the 'Jolly Roger' flag after a successful mission to sink the supply ship *Barenfels* at Bergen, Norway, September 1944. The vessel was also used in the attack on a floating dock at Bergen on 11 September 1944. *X24* is preserved at the RNSM, Gosport.** *(RNSM)*

D Day - the day on which the midgets were to be slipped by their towing submarines- was fixed provisionally for the 20 September.

'Alternative operation orders were prepared for attacks on Alten fjord in the extreme north (Operation 'Funnel'), on the Narvik area-between latitude (lat.) 67° and 69° N. (Operation 'Empire'), and on Trondheim between lat. 63° and 65° N (Operation 'Forced') so that operations could be directed against the enemy in whichever area he might be located. In the event this proved to be Alten fjord (Operation 'Funnel').

'Six operational submarines with the X-craft in tow were to proceed independently to a position 75 miles (120.7km) west of the Shetlands and then to follow routes some 20 miles (32.3km) apart until about 150 miles (241.4km) from Alten fjord, when they were to steer for positions from which to make their landfalls.

'The operational crews were to take over the X-craft from the passage crews at any time convenient after D Day-3 (17 September)'. The planners then gave each operational submarine a sector to seaward

Right: ***X5* was launched at the Royal Navy's base at Faslane, Scotland on 31 December 1942.** *(RNSM)*

Above & left:
The side charges (mines) as fitted to the X-craft for the *Tirpitz* attack. Each weighed 4 tons (4,064kg) and contained 2 tons (2,032kg) of Amatex explosive to be detonated by clock timer fuses. Amatex, a highly sensitive explosive, consisted of 40% RDX, 40% TNT and 20% ammonium nitrate. The charges were in three parts; the centre section contained the explosive. *(RNSM)*

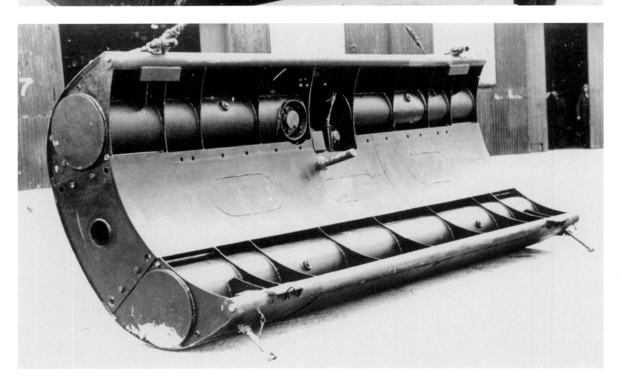

Right: **Lt. Terry-Lloyd RN, Commanding Officer of the passage crew in** *X5*, **assists a fellow officer in exiting the W&D compartment on an X-craft. The only vessel in the X-20 series to be lost was** *X22*, **which was involved in a collision during a towing excercise with S-class HMS/m** *Syrtis*, **7 February 1944.** *(RNSM)*

of the declared mined area off Soroy Sound in which to patrol after making landfall. The X-craft were to be slipped from the tow in positions 2 to 5 miles (3.22km to 9km) from the mined area after dusk on D Day (20 September), when the craft would cross the mined area on the surface and proceed via Stjernsund to Alten fjord, submerging during daylight hours on 21 September. All were to arrive off the entrance to Kaafjord at dawn on 22 September, and then, entering the Fleet anchorage, attack the targets for which each craft had been detailed. These would be allocated by signal during the passage, in the light of the most recent intelligence'.

The Battle Summary continued: 'As soon as the X-craft were slipped, the operational submarines were to return to their patrol sectors, and to remain in them during the operations of the X-craft in the fjords. To facilitate the recovery of the midgets, each operational submarine had been supplied with three infra-red transmitters and the X-craft with special-type receivers. Those which were able to withdraw after the attack were to endeavour to contact a submarine in one of the sectors, in each of which a 'Recovery' position had been established. Should this fail they were to make for one of the bays on the north coast of the island of Soroy to the west of Hammerfast, which, circumstances permitting, would be closed and examined by some of the operational submarines on the nights of the 27/28 and 28/29 September'. The X-craft commanders were also told that should they not be recovered

Kaafjord photographed from a high-flying reconnaissance aircraft based in Russia. The main anti-torpedo boom defence is visible at the top of the photograph, with *Tirpitz* (bottom left) surrounded by additional anti-torpedo defences. *(RNSM)*

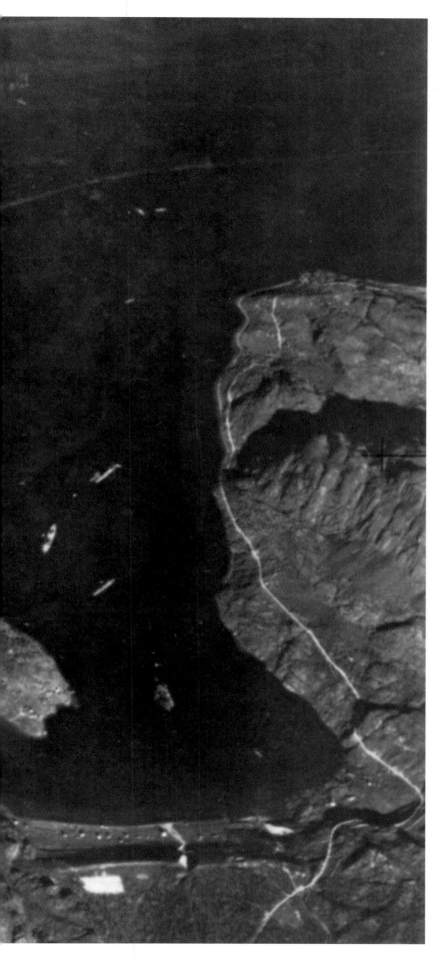

from the vicinity of Soroy they could then make their way around North Cape to Kola Inlet, Murmansk, Russia. The Senior British Naval Officer, North Russia, was requested to arrange for a minesweeper to keep a look out for midget submarines from 25 September to 3 October. It was essential that the planners should have preliminary and the latest photo-reconnaissance in case targets moved or there were changes to net defences and anything else that might hazard the operation. Here again, the planning was very thorough.

A photographic unit was sent in the destroyers HMS *Musketeer* and HMS *Mahratta* to Murmansk in northern Russia. The Alten area was beyond aircraft based in Britain and so a 'shuttle' service of De Havilland Mosquito aircraft was used for the preliminary tasks and the Supermarine Spitfires for the last-minute sorties, operating from Vaenga, now the Russian naval base of Severomorsk, 16 miles (26 km) from Murmansk on the Kola Inlet. Bad weather hampered Mosquito operations but Admiral Barry reported that the operations by three Spitfires proved invaluable. These aircraft were from No. 543 Squadron, a photo-reconnaissance unit formed on 19 October 1942 at Benson, Oxfordshire equipped with Spitfires, initially the Mk IV and V and from September 1943 the Mk XI.

One of No. 543's missions in 1943 was to take photographs of the results of the Dams Raid in Germany by No. 617 Squadron on 16 May. Also No. 543 carried both the pre and post mission sorties against the *Tirpitz*. Intelligence on the enemy movements was signalled to the X-craft crews before they left …a few hours before the first photographs were received. This did not cause any concern as the signalled information was good. There was comforting intelligence with coded messages from brave Norwegian resistance members. One of those courageous men was Torstein Raaby, who took incredible risks by using his next door German neighbour's transmitter aerial for sending

*Above: **Tirpitz** surrounded by camouflage barges and supply vessels, the location is Fæhenfjord, Norway, 16 January1942. (IWM)*

Left: An oblique view aerial reconnaissance photograph taken by an aircraft based in Russia. The German Navy thought the difficult to navigate location would deter any attack. (IWM)

Above: **The location of *Tirpitz* in Kaafjord before the attack by X-craft.** *(IWM)*

Right: **Photographed from a Spitfire aircraft flying at 200ft, this shows detail of the deck area aft of the funnel on *Tirpitz*.** *(IWM)*

Operation 'Source' crews were:
Passage Crew

X5
Lieutenant J.V. Terry Lloyd, SANF
Acting Leading Seaman B.W. Element
Stoker 1st class N. Garrity

X6
Lieutenant A. Wilson RNVR
Leading Seaman J. J. McGregor
Stoker 1st class W. Oakley

X7
Lieutenant P.H. Philip SANF (V)
Able Seaman 3rd class J. Magennis
Stoker 1st class F. Luck

Operational Crew

X5
Lieutenant H. Henty-Creer, RNVR
Midshipman D.J. Malcolm, RNVR
Sub Lieutenant T.J. Nelson, RNVR
Engine Room Artificer 4th class J.J. Mortiboys

X6
Lieutenant D. Cameron, RNR
Sub Lieutenant J. T. Lorimer, RNVR
Sub Lieutenant R.H. Kendall, RNVR
Engine Room Artificer 4th class E. Goddard

X7
Lieutenant B. C. G. Place, DSC, RN
Sub Lieutenant B. Whittam, RNVR
Sub Lieutenant R. Aitken, RNVR
Engine Room Artificer 4th class M. Whitley

his own messages to Britain! (Raaby was later a crew member when, in 1947, Thor Heyerdahl made his classic voyage on the balsa logs raft *Kon-Tiki* from the western coast of Peru to Polynesia). Apart from the 'spotting' help provided by Raaby and his equally brave friends, there was the photographic evidence that *Tirpitz* and the 26,000-ton battle cruiser *Scharnhorst* were anchored in Kaafjord and the armoured ship (more popularly known as 'pocket battleship') *Lutzow* was in nearby Langefjord. The midget submarines were to attack all three - and this is a point survivors of the assault make - *Tirpitz* was not the only target. In April 1944 *Lutzow*, along with another pocket battleship, *Admiral Scheer* was badly damaged by RAF bombing while in Kiel. In May that year *Lutzow* was scuttled.

The three German warships were to be attacked as follows:

X5, *X6* and *X7* - *Tirpitz*, *X9* and *X10* – *Scharnhorst* and *X8* - *Lutzow*.

The submarines selected for towing duties required a depot ship and on 30 August 1943 the 5,200 ton HMS *Titania*

(commanded by Cdr. W. R. Fell, OBE, DSC, RN, ret.) arrived at Loch Cairnbawn. HM Submarines *Thrasher* (Lt. A. R. Hezlet DSC, RN), *Truculent* (Lt. R. L. Alexander DSO, RN), *Stubborn* (Lt. A. A. Duff, RN), *Seanymph* (Lt. J. P. H. Oakley DSC,RN), *Syrtis* (Lt. M. H. Jupp DSC,RN) and *Sceptre* (Lt. I. McIntosh, RN) soon arrived. The towing arrangements were: *Thrasher - X5*; *Truculent - X6*; *Stubborn - X7*; *Seanymph - X8*; *Syrtis - X9* and *Sceptre - X10*.

Starting on the afternoon of 11 September 1943, the T and S class submarines began towing the X-craft on the long journey to the Arctic circle and the first four days have been described as uneventful. It is unlikely the crews being towed would describe the experience in that manner. Initially, the towing submarines travelled on the surface at between eight and 10 knots, the X-craft being approximately 40 to 50ft (12 to 15m) below the waves.

The X-craft had to surface every six hours to change the air in the cramped conditions, to charge batteries and, if need be, recharge air bottles as well. Even though

Passage Crew

X8
Lieutenant J. Smart RNVR
Acting Leading Seaman A.H. Harte
Stoker 1st class G. Robinson

X9
Sub Lieutenant E. Kearon RNVR
Able Seaman A.H. Harte
Stoker 1st class H. Hollet

X10
Sub Lieutenant E.V. Page, RNVR
Engine Room Artificer 4th class H.J. Fishleigh
Acting Petty Officer A. Brookes

Operational Crew

X8
Lieutenant B.M. McFarlane, RAN
Lieutenant W.J. Marsden, RANVR
Sub Lieutenant R. Hindmarsh, RN
Engine Room Artificer 4th class J.B. Murrary

X9
Lieutenant T.L. Martin, RN
Sub Lieutenant J. Brooks, RN
Lieutenant M. Shean, RANVR
Engine Room Artificer 4th class V. Coles

X10
Lieutenant K. Hudspeth, RANVR
Sub Lieutenant B.E. Enzer, RNVR
Midshipman G.G. Harding, RNVR
Engine Room Artificer 4th class L. Tilley

the weather was good at the start, the feeling of movement has been likened to 'porpoising' rather than pitching or rolling and on 15 September came the first sign of trouble for the passage crews. The weather turned really nasty and the telephone link between *Seanymph* and *X8* failed. Even worse, at around 0400 hours the tow parted. The question of tow ropes will be the subject of further attention and is still a subject for discussion by veterans. It was 36 hours - without communication - before *Seanymph* recovered the missing X-craft, and the operational crew relieved their passage shipmates who were by then well and truly fatigued. Fighting the awful conditions and concentrating hard on their various duties was extremely demanding for the passage crews without whom the operation could not have had any chance of success. They may not have expected to face the might of the German Navy, but they discovered on 15 September that danger had certainly entered into the equation. Sleep, real sleep was as elusive as real exercise and hot food was the contents from several tins mixed together and heated in a

carpenter's glue pot. Richard Compton-Hall in his book *Submarine Warfare: Monsters and Midgets* credits Able Seaman 'Mick' Magennis of *X7's* passage crew as being an 'excellent' chef. Magennis, as a Leading Seaman, went on to be awarded the Victoria Cross in *XE3* - so did his commanding officer Lt. Ian. E. Fraser, RNR for the raid in Singapore harbour, 31 July 1945. Hot food could only be cooked when the X-craft were on the surface, to prevent steam from adding to the condensation problems of the interior.

The troubles of *X8* were not over - and for the crew of *X9* the ultimate nightmare occurred on the morning of 16 September when the tow rope parted. The crew of *Syrtis* discovered the problem when SUE charges (Signal Underwater Exploding – similar to a small hand grenade) were dropped - a signal for *X9's* crew to surface for the regular 'breather' (fresh air). There was no response and it was later assumed the weight of the manila rope, now sodden with sea water, was heavy enough to drag *X9* down - together with three brave men.

Sub-Lieutenant Kearon, Able Seaman Harte and Stoker 1st Class Hollett were

Left: **Submarine Depot Ship HMS** *Titania* **moored in Loch Cairnbawn with a submarine alongside.** *Titania* **was required to service the submarines chosen for the long tow to Norway. The vessel arrived at the Loch on 30 August 1943.** *(RNSM)*

never seen again. All were entered in official reports named as 'Lost on Passage'. Back to the problems for the crew of *X8* where, on the morning of the 17 September the starboard side cargo was losing air - meaning difficulties in trying to maintain trim - and was jettisoned. Later that day, at 1630, Lt. McFarlane decided that to keep the midget submarine level he would have to jettison the port cargo. The charge released in 180 fathoms (490m), set to detonate two hours after being jettisoned to give *Seanymph* and the towed *X8* plenty of time to clear the area. Unfortunately, after approximately one hour and 45 minutes the charge exploded and amazingly (*X8* just 3 miles (4.8km) away) caused flooding in the W&D compartment, and damaged pipework, leaving the craft in no state to continue. With the operational crew safely extricated it was decided that *X8* was to be scuttled. Now, two of the six craft in the attack plan were out of action, both had suffered tow rope failures. On 20 September the situation could have become worse but for some very nimble footwork by Lt. Place on *X7*. He fended off a mine, gently nudging it away aft with his feet!

The tow ropes feature prominently in the memories of the Operation 'Source' men. John Lorimer stated: 'None of the craft had been at sea for more than about five continuous days. We were being towed for ten days, by which time things had gone wrong and we'd lost two of the X-craft because of tow ropes'. Vernon Coles told the author: 'With the loss of *X9* the first feelings of the operational crew were those of sadness at the loss of our passage crew – Sub-Lt. 'Paddy' Kearon, Able Seaman 'Darkie' Harte, and Stoker 'Ginger' Hollett'. All three were close friends of Coles, especially Hollett. 'He and I were the only two engine room people in the crews and he was a bubbly fellow, full of life and always working, doing something for the betterment of the boat. Feelings then turned to the deepest disappointment and to anger because the RN had failed to give us adequate tow ropes; particularly as we were sailing on the greatest submarine attack ever'. Coles also said: 'Our manila tow ropes broke right, left and centre (regularly) in training, even though they were specially made for the job.

'The towing submarine and X-craft were in telephone communication, or should have been, at all times - the telephone cable

Above: **The only photograph of an X-craft under tow on the voyage to Norwegian waters and Operation 'Source'. HMS/m** *Thrasher,* **a T-class submarine with** *X5.* **Two T-class and four S-class vessels were used.** *(RNSM)*

ran up the centre of the tow rope. But the tow rope stretched and the telephone cables didn't, so that was a problem. Then, when we got hold of a nylon tow rope, we had no trouble whatsoever. You can imagine the surprise when there were only three nylon tow ropes available for the final operation; they went to *X5, X6* and *X10.* We knew very well that we didn't have a tow rope which would last any more than five days but we were told not to worry because the towing submarine had a spare cable. It's all very well to change a tow rope when you're on a canoe lake at Portsmouth, but when you're out in the middle of the North Sea getting close to the Arctic Circle it's quite a problem - you've only got 18 inches (46 cm) free board above the water line. Godfrey Place (CO *X7*) achieved it. He had the broken tow rope replaced, then the second tow rope only lasted two days and finished by towing with a steel cable and still got there on time. That was a remarkable effort'.

The alternative materiel to manila was nylon; costly, and in short supply. Lt. Cameron (CO *X6*) had insisted on a nylon tow rope and it proved a very wise decision. Tow ropes were just one of several problems

that emerged prior to the start of the attack on *Tirpitz.* Robert Aitken, reminiscing in 2005, told the author that although training had been extended to autumn because the crews were not ready in March – 'I am still not convinced we were ready in the autumn'. He was at the helm one night when Lt. Place gave the order 'dive, dive, dive' and Sub Lt. Aitken was still fumbling with the valves when Place came to the rescue. 'It occurred to me afterwards that though I had taken control of the valves in the light, I had never done so in the dark'. He is also of the opinion that the sense of urgency brought about by wartime means almost inevitable technical problems - and that a lot depends in operations on luck - good or bad.

On the evening of 20 September, between 1830 and 2000 hours, *X5, X6, X7* and *X10* cast off from the towing submarines and headed towards the minefields protecting the entry to Altenfjord. Having negotiated this hazard successfully, the craft moved to the small island of Tommelholm, near the entry point for Kaafjord. At dawn on the next day, 21 September 1943, the craft would be ready for the attack and in position by dusk.

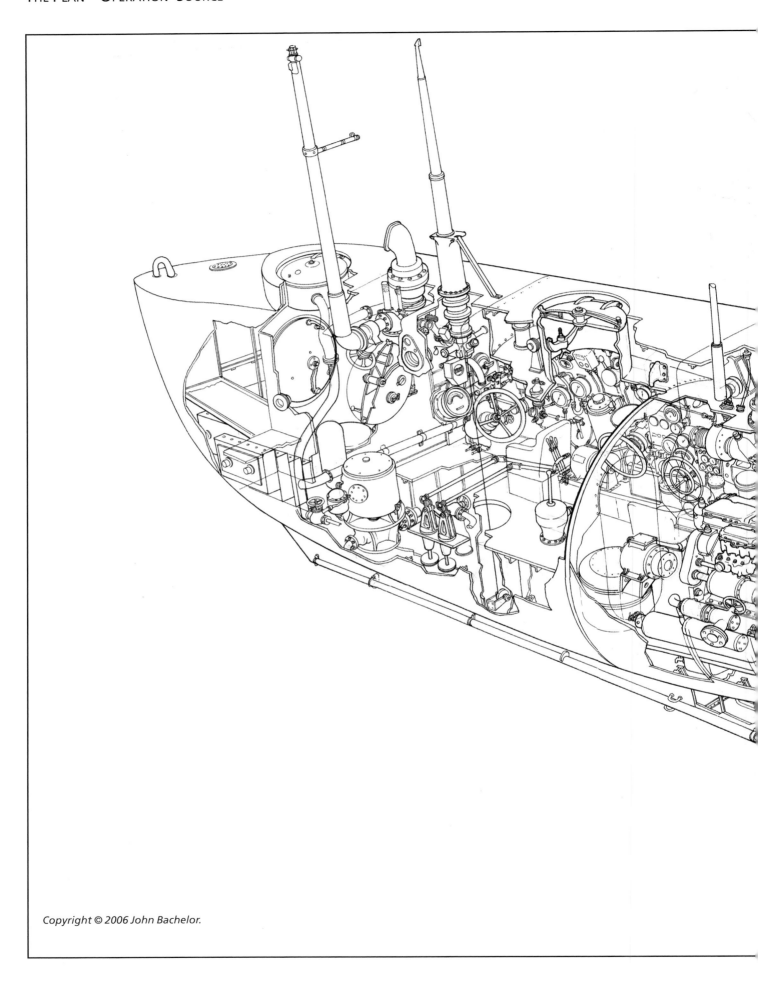

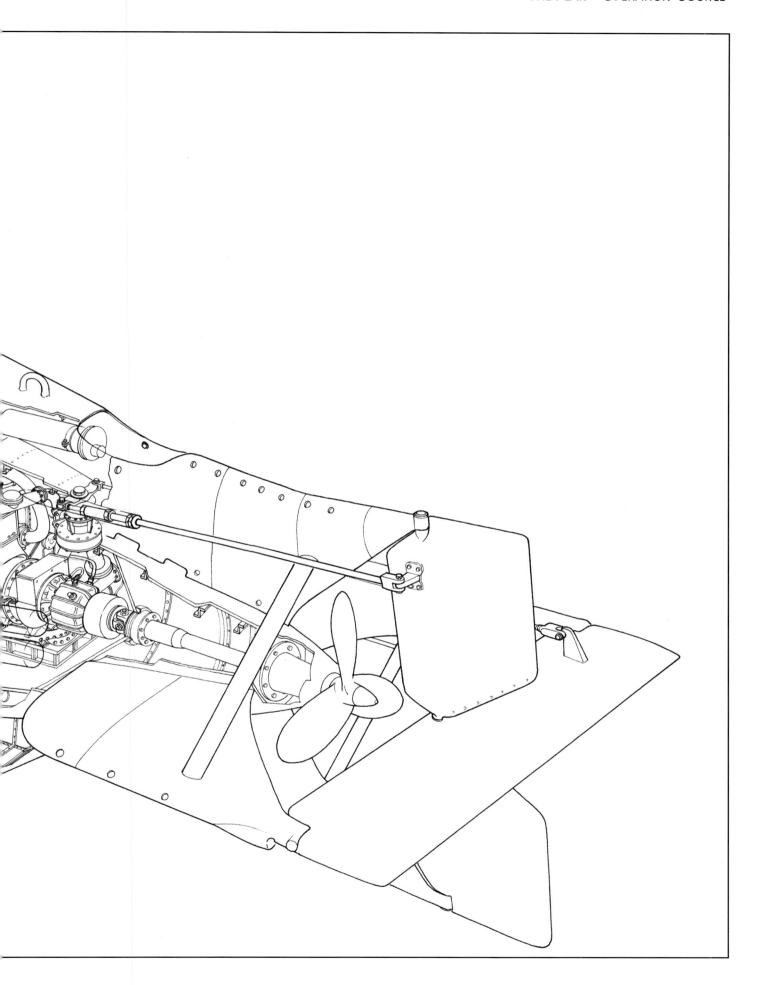

Although all the X-craft were
lost during Operation 'Source',
of the 42 officers and men in
the crews, 33 were to survive

4

THE ATTACK

The 16 crewmen of the four remaining X-craft were ready for the task at hand. They were trained, they were fit and they were confident. They had the benefit of weather conditions ideal for their craft and themselves, according to the Australian Lt. Ken Hudspeth, RANVR, CO of *X10*. The battle summary said the sky was 'dull, and overcast and a fresh breeze raising white horses to assist an unseen attack'. Hudspeth did not know at that point that his target, *Scharnhorst*, was at sea. The crew of *Tirpitz* did not have a clue that their world was to receive a severe

shaking and they no doubt felt comfortable behind the anti-submarine net at the entrance to Kaafjord, and the three anti-torpedo nets, descending, it was thought by naval intelligence, to approximately 40ft (12m) beneath the surface. The battle summary points out that in order to allow all X-craft ample time to reach their objectives, and to guard against the loss of surprise through one of them attacking prematurely, 'they had been forbidden to attack before 0100, 22 September, but they were free to do so at any time after that, setting their charges

Left: **Even
operating the
Barr & Stroud
miniature in the
close confines of
an X-craft was
difficult.** *(RNSM)*

Right: **The trim control position in an X-craft.** *(IWM)*

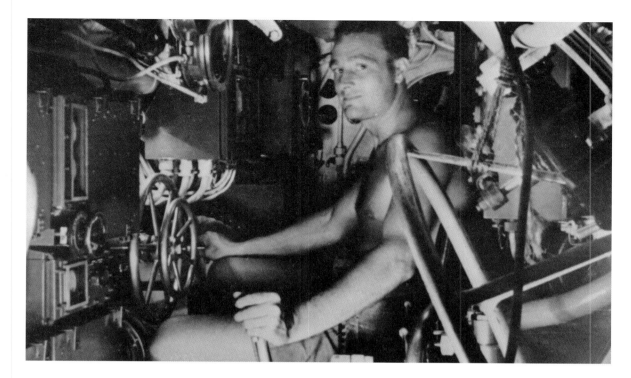

Below: **One of the X-craft used in the attack on *Tirpitz*. HMS/m *X10* is here leaving her mooring buoy in Loch Cairnbawn.** *(NMM)*

to explode in accordance with a 'firing rules table' given in the operation orders'. Actually, the commanding officers had agreed between themselves to make their attacks between 0500 and 0800, laying the charges set to fire at 0830, by which time it was hoped that they would have been able to withdraw from the area.

Bearing in mind that Battle Summary No.29 was based on reports up to and including December 1944, when six surviving personnel of the attack on *Tirpitz* were still in a German Prisoner-of-War camp, the report got most of the basic information right and

it is worth looking at the brevity of the record of those astonishing events. It credits Lt. Donald Cameron and his crew in *X6* with being first on the scene in Kaafjord. 'At some time unknown, her periscope had become flooded, and the Commanding Officer was therefore completely 'blind' with no means of conning his craft when dived.

Having got past the anti-submarine net and entered the fleet anchorage, Lieutenant Cameron, with a complete disregard for danger, proceeded on the surface in broad daylight astern of a small coaster through the

boat entrance in the nets, situated only 200 yd (183m) away from the *Tirpitz*. After passing safely through the boat entrance at about 0800, *X6* was sighted close on the port bow of the *Tirpitz*, and as she dived was attacked with hand grenades thrown from the upper deck of the battleship, while a pinnace started to drop depth charges. Lieutenant Cameron pressed home his attack, and released one charge probably while passing under the bridge of the *Tirpitz*, then, failing to turn to starboard quickly enough, he fouled the nets to starboard of her and was forced to go astern to get clear. In doing so he hit the *Tirpitz*, and as he knew he had been sighted he released his second charge and then surfaced almost alongside. After seeing all his crew (Sub Lieutenants Lorimer and Kendall and Engine Room Artificer Goddard) safely out of *X6*, he scuttled her; all were picked up and taken on board the *Tirpitz*. This was at approximately 0805'. To reduce what was high drama and excitement to the official matter-of-fact account was standard service reporting. Despite the towing and technical problems, Lorimer still thinks the X-craft 'was an incredible weapon and hopefully Operation 'Source' proved its worth. The *Tirpitz*, our target was the most magnificent ship I'd ever seen. It seemed an awful pity to blow her up'. One subsequent

account claims Lorimer 'threw a smart one' (salute) on boarding the great battleship. Not so. 'I stood to attention, having lost my cap', he confirmed to the author. He also confirmed that the four crewmen of *X6* were well treated by the Germans on capture, the mood changed after the explosions and the captain of *Tirpitz* did threaten to have them shot at one stage.

Perhaps the sighting of *X6* proved a distraction at the right time. Lt. Godfrey Place in *X7* pressed on with the attack and, says the battle summary: 'Having penetrated the anti-submarine net at the entrance to Kaafjord, Lieutenant Place manoeuvred to pass under the close anti-torpedo nets. Here he had an unpleasant surprise; instead of the expected gap under them, he found that they extended 120ft (37m) below the surface, which meant that they were practically on the bottom.

'Undeterred by this, at his third attempt he managed to worm *X7* along the bottom under the nets. Lieutenant Place laid one of his charges under the *Tirpitz's* funnel and the other under her after turret, apparently undetected, and was then faced with the task of again negotiating the nets to make his escape. To add to his difficulties the tide was ebbing and there was even less space under the nets than before. Before long *X7* was once again foul of them; she was only about 170ft (52m)

Above: **X-craft were towed to Norway behind submarines, two were T-class. Illustrated is HMS/m *Torbay*, a T-class vessel moored at Barry, South Wales prior to being scrapped in 1945.** *(RNSM)*

Above: **Four of the X-craft used in the attack were towed by S-class submarines. This is HMS/m** *Shakespeare*, **an S-class vessel built in 1940. The vessel is departing Algiers, Morocco in 1943.** *(RNSM)*

from the line on which the charges had been laid, and the time for the explosion was drawing nearer every minute. Eventually she cleared the nets and was some 400yd (366m) to seaward of them when at 0830 the explosion took place. At this distance the force of the explosions so damaged *X7* as to put her out of action, and Lieutenant Place decided to remain on the bottom to await events. About an hour later he realised the extent of the damage and that nothing more could be done. By this time the operation was compromised; depth charges were being dropped indiscriminately about the fjord, though up to that point not particularly near to *X7*, and he decided to surface to give his crew a chance of escaping. As soon as she appeared on the surface, she was hotly engaged by gunfire and sunk. Two of her crew (Sub Lieutenant Whittam and Engine Room Artificer Whitley) were lost. Lieutenant Place and Sub Lieutenant Aitken, the third officer, escaped and were rescued by the Germans; they were taken on board the *Tirpitz,* where they found the crew of *X6* being questioned by officers of the Admiral's staff. All of them were well treated and given hot coffee and schnapps; great admiration for their bravery was expressed by the enemy'. Place told John Stretton of *The News,* Portsmouth's evening newspaper, in September 1976: 'I

knew that both of the charges, mine and Cameron's had gone off. But Cameron didn't know then that the big explosion which had rocked the ship included my charges, as well as his. I'm blessed if I know why it was not enough to sink her. The probable explanation was that the force of the explosion blew off part of the charges'.

'Escaped and rescued by Germans' is perhaps the minimum officialese for the drama that faced Place's three crewmen. When the Germans opened fire on *X7,* Robert Aitken recalled: 'Fortunately we were too close to the *Tirpitz* to enable her heavy armament to fire at us. The CO opened the W&D hatch, waving a rather dirty white sweater to indicate surrender. The small arms fire stopped but as the CO climbed onto the casing he realised we were about to hit a moored target and with the hatch open the boat, with little buoyancy, would be flooded. He turned round to shut the hatch, which I was trying to push open from below and quite a bit of water came in before the hatch was closed. It was enough to sink the boat, which plunged to the bottom'. The author asked Robert Aitken if thoughts of potential disaster had crossed his mind during training. 'No', he said, adding with a smile: 'I was never blessed with a good imagination, fortunately'. He compared the attitude of most

Above: **Tirpitz** at her moorings in Kaafjord before the attack by X-craft on 22 September 1943. *(JA)*

Left: **The Barr & Stroud miniature periscope.** *(RNSM)*

Above: **The area of Kaafjord, as it is today, where** *Tirpitz* **was moored.** *(JA)*

of his friends in World War Two to today's young and enthusiastic motorcyclists. 'It (an accident) is never going to happen to you, is it?' The three left on board were apprehensive about trying to get the boat to the surface because it had been damaged and using compressors and motors would mean noise which, in turn, could bring depth charges. 'We decided that it would be wiser to escape using the breathing apparatus. We all put one on and started to flood the boat (the hatch could not be opened until the boat was fully flooded to equalise the pressure inside the boat with that outside). Unfortunately this took longer than we anticipated because some of the valves could not be fully opened. As the water crept up it reached the batteries which fused, giving off fumes, and we had to start breathing oxygen before the boat was fully flooded'. Aitken does remember thinking 'this could not happen to me. This was an optimistic, not pessimistic, thought', he told me. After discovering ERA Bill Whitley was dead, the pressure equalised 'just after I'd broken my first emergency bottle. I opened the hatch, climbed out and jumped'.

'As the pressure began to reduce, the oxygen expanded, leaving me with far too much. I made what I thought was a correct escape. I unrolled and held out the apron (provided with the escape kit for use as a brake) so I didn't go up too fast and blow out my lungs, and thinking how pleased Chads (Warrant Officer Chadwick, my diving instructor) would have been to see me doing what I was told'. As the sixth survivor of the attack, Aitken had hoped to find a seventh on the surface. It was not to be. There was no sign of Sub Lt. Whittam. Then Aitken saw the *Tirpitz*: 'it was a great disappointment to see her afloat. She was very large, the pride of the German Navy, and I had been very hopeful she had been sunk, but she looked intact from my limited viewpoint'.

But what of *X5* and *X10*? The part played by *X5*, commanded by Lieutenant Henty Henty-Creer is not known, said the battle summary. Sixty years after the end of World War Two the mystery has still not been solved

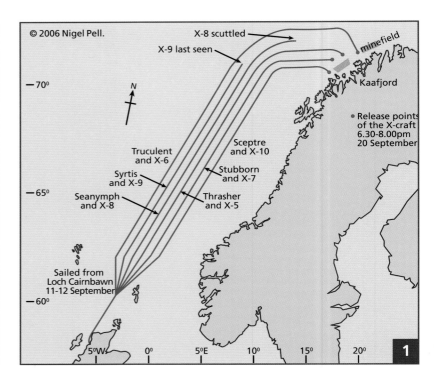

Operation 'Source'
The X-craft's routes and attack on the *Tirpitz*, 20-28 September 1943

Map 1. Route of X-craft and towing submarines from Loch Cairnbawn to Kaafjord.

Map 2. Route of X-craft into Kaafjord and X-10's return route.

Map 3. Route of X-6 and X-7 , Kaafjord, 22 September 1943.

Map 4. The attack on the *Tirpitz* , Kaafjord, 22 September 1943.

© 2006 Nigel Pell.

X-8 scuttled
X-9 last seen
minefield
Kaafjord

Release points of the X-craft 6.30-8.00pm 20 September

Truculent and X-6
Sceptre and X-10
Syrtis and X-9
Stubborn and X-7
Seanymph and X-8
Thrasher and X-5

Sailed from Loch Cairnbawn 11-12 September

5°W 0° 5°E 10° 15° 20°

1

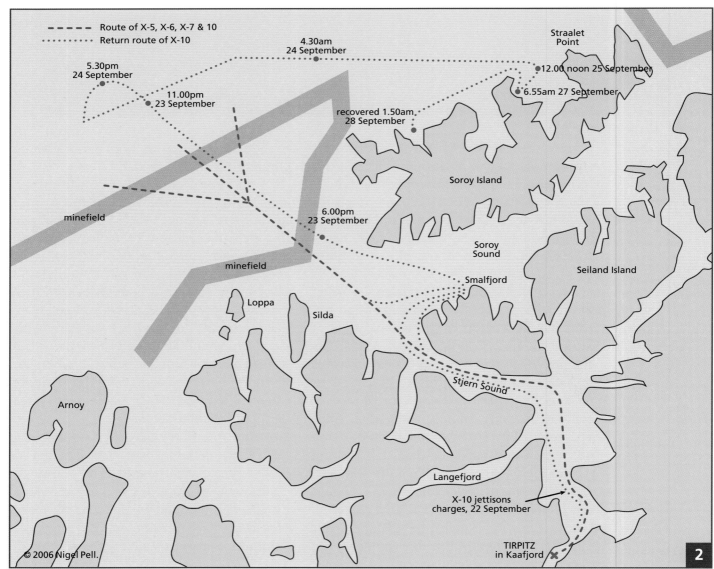

Route of X-5, X-6, X-7 & 10
Return route of X-10

5.30pm 24 September
4.30am 24 September
Straalet Point
11.00pm 23 September
12.00 noon 25 September
6.55am 27 September
recovered 1.50am 28 September
Soroy Island
minefield
6.00pm 23 September
Soroy Sound
minefield
Seiland Island
Smalfjord
Loppa
Silda
Stjern Sound
Arnoy
Langefjord
X-10 jettisons charges, 22 September
TIRPITZ in Kaafjord

© 2006 Nigel Pell.

2

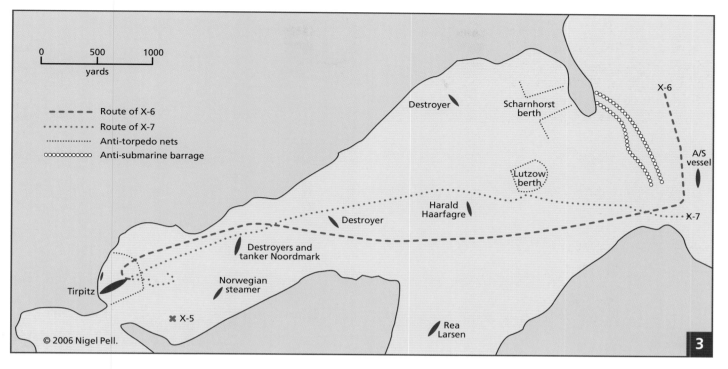

Route of X-6
Route of X-7
Anti-torpedo nets
Anti-submarine barrage

Destroyer

Scharnhorst berth

X-6

A/S vessel

Lutzow berth

Harald Haarfagre

X-7

Destroyer

Destroyers and tanker Noordmark

Norwegian steamer

Tirpitz

X-5

Rea Larsen

© 2006 Nigel Pell.

3

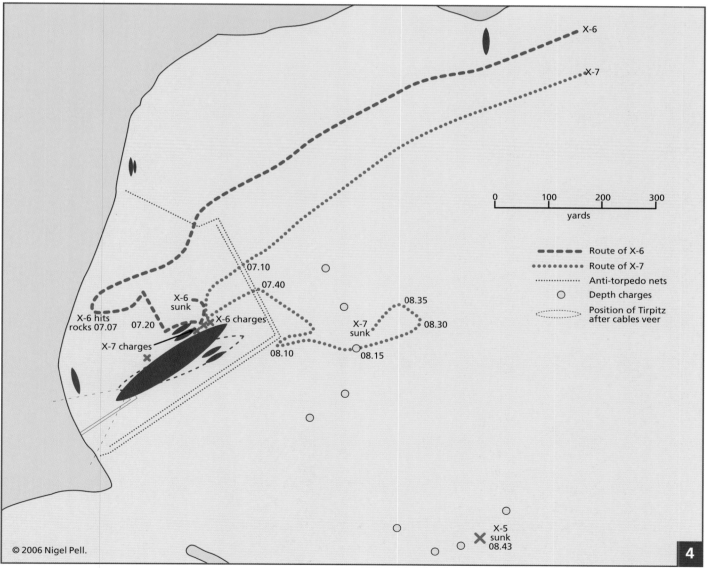

X-6

X-7

0   100   200   300
yards

Route of X-6
Route of X-7
Anti-torpedo nets
Depth charges
Position of Tirpitz after cables veer

07.10

07.40

X-6 sunk

08.35

X-6 charges

08.30

X-7 sunk

X-6 hits rocks 07.07

07.20

08.10

08.15

X-7 charges

X-5 sunk 08.43

© 2006 Nigel Pell.

4

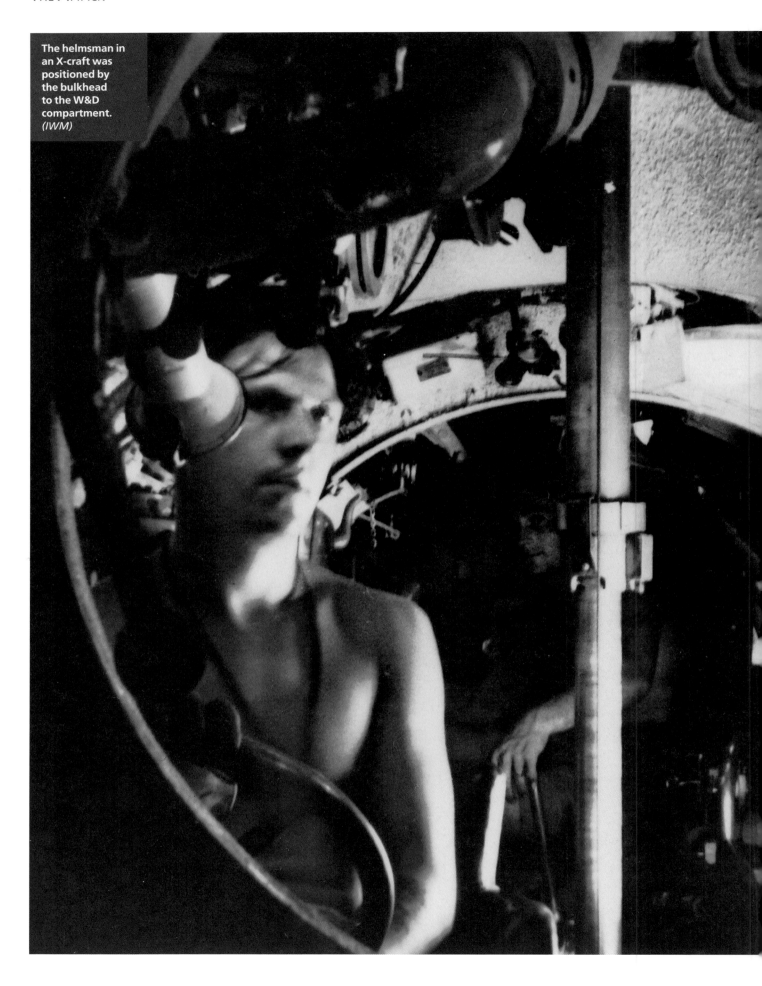

The helmsman in an X-craft was positioned by the bulkhead to the W&D compartment. *(IWM)*

and the absence of awards for *X5* crew, above those of Mentioned in Despatches, remains the subject of controversy. The battle summary states: 'Some time after the attack, divers found wreckage – presumably from this craft – about one mile (1.6km) to seaward of the *Tirpitz*, halfway between her and the entrance to Kaafjord. No bodies or personal gear was found, and of survivors there was not a trace. It is believed that she was destroyed by depth charges; whether she was on her way out at the time, after laying her charges, or whether she was waiting to go in during the next attacking period (i.e., after 0900) will very possibly never be known'. In the case of *X10*, the summary could be more detailed because Lt Hudspeth and his crew survived to tell the tale - which is one filled with frustration. 'The first signs of trouble occurred at 0110, 22 September, when it was realised that the gyro compass was wandering', the summary states. Thirty minutes later *X10* dived to avoid being seen by a vessel approaching from ahead.

It was then found that the damping bottles of the gyro compass were not working, and on raising the projector compass the light failed to function. As this light could only be replaced by removing the top cover from outside, *X10* was left with no compass at all. Worse was to follow. 'At 0150 she came to periscope depth, and on attempting to raise the periscope a fire developed from the periscope hoisting motor, and Lieutenant Hudspeth was obliged to surface to ventilate and clear her of fumes. Dawn was then breaking, and *X10* was almost within sight of the entrance of Kaafjord. Clearly, with no compass and with no means of raising or lowering her periscope, she was in no condition to carry out the attack, and Lieutenant Hudspeth decided to bottom before daylight set in'. *X10* remained on the seabed during daylight on 22 September, whilst the crew were trying to solve the problem of the defects. At 0830 two very heavy explosions were heard at intervals of a few seconds and after a further five minutes later, nine further heavy explosions were heard at short, irregular intervals. These were followed between 0900 and 1000 by a burst of around 12 lighter explosions, repeated louder and closer about 1100.

Left: **A painting by Lt. D. A. Rapkins, RN of the X-craft's diver cutting through anti-torpedo netting. The diver's suit was a development of the 'Sladen suit' designed by Commander G. M. Sladen, DSO, DSC, RN, originally for charioteers. It was officially known as the Admiralty Pattern Shallow Water Diving Dress.** *(RNSM)*

Left: **The Starkie Gardner net cutter. This was worked by water and air pressure from the X-craft through flexible pipes. The equipment was designed to be operated in one hand.** *(RNSM)*

DETAILS OF THE NETS RIGGED AROUND TIRPITZ IN KAAFJORD.

ELEVATION OF NETS.

SECTIONAL VIEW.

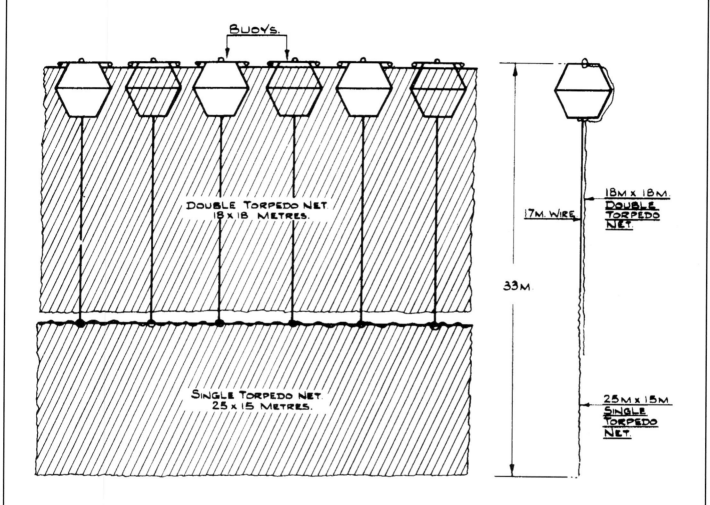

BUOYS.

DOUBLE TORPEDO NET.
18 x 18 METRES.

SINGLE TORPEDO NET.
25 x 15 METRES.

18M x 18M.
DOUBLE
TORPEDO
NET.

17M. WIRE.

33M.

25M x 15M.
SINGLE
TORPEDO
NET.

PLAN VIEW.

BUOY ON LEFT AND BUOY ON RIGHT OF NET ALTERNATELY

ADMIRALTY
D.N.C. DEPT.
N6/A66
N H
FEBRUARY 1948

PREPARED FROM
INFORMATION SUPPLIED
BY N.I.D.

Left: Taken from the deck of *Tirpitz* this picture shows the splashes from gunfire directed at *X7* as it surfaced close by the gunnery target, at left. *(JA)*

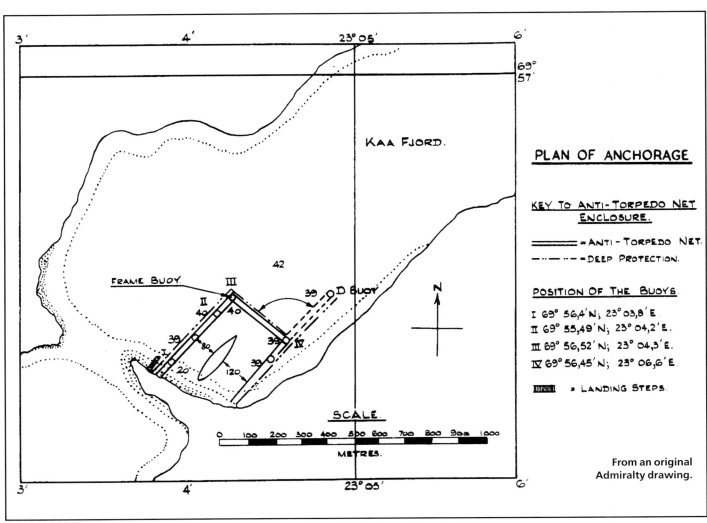

KAA FJORD.

FRAME BUOY

III

II

39 D BUOY

I

PLAN OF ANCHORAGE

KEY TO ANTI-TORPEDO NET ENCLOSURE.

═══════ = ANTI-TORPEDO NET.

—·—·— = DEEP PROTECTION.

POSITION OF THE BUOYS.

I   69° 56,4′ N; 23° 03,8′ E.
II 69° 55,49′ N; 23° 04,2′ E.
III 69° 56,52′ N; 23° 04,3′ E.
IV 69° 56,45′ N; 23° 06,6′ E.

▦▦▦ = LANDING STEPS.

SCALE.

0 100 200 300 400 500 600 700 800 900 1000

METRES.

From an original Admiralty drawing.

Above: **The scene of the sinking of *X7* as it is today.** *(JA)*

That afternoon with the defects in *X10* still not rectified and being convinced by the explosions that the attack had been carried out, Lieutenant Hudspeth reluctantly decided to give up any idea of attacking, and at 1800 surfaced and made for deep water. At 1825 both charges, set to 'safe', were jettisoned in 135 fathoms (247m), and *X10* then proceeded on main engine out of Altenfjord. More equipment problems followed, after the light in the projector compass had been replaced and with the periscope lashed in the 'up' position, a rendezvous with *Stubborn* was made and the transfer of the crew was effected at 2200 on 29 September. 'By this time the operational crew had been on board their craft for almost exactly 10 days. They had been subjected to much hardship, discomfort and disappointment, but were none the worse for their experience', the battle summary recorded.

That was not the end of the problems with *X10*. On the return journey to Scotland there were more problems with the tow, and on 2 October with *Stubborn* still 400 miles (644km) from Lerwick and a gale threatening, the decision was taken to recover the passage crew and sink *X10*. So not one of the six midget craft deployed for the attack would return. There was some relief amid the sense of loss for those who had died that casualties were not proportionate to the loss of X-craft. Of the 42 officers and men who crewed the midget submarines, 33 survived. Three men were lost on passage and six to enemy action.

For the six men now prisoners on board *Tirpitz* after the attack, there must have been nervousness on two counts - how would the Germans treat them? (It was known that after the previous raid surviving charioteer, Able Seaman Bob Evans, had been shot as a spy when captured). Or would they be injured from the charges they had laid? At about 0812 came the explosions and the answers. Though one German seaman was killed and 40 injured, the British escaped injury. The *Tirpitz* was badly damaged. The hull was intact, if showing a few cracks, but such was the power of the blast that there was considerable shock damage to turbine mountings, engine and condenser casing and two of the three propeller shafts could not be turned. The steering compartment was flooded and four gun turrets were lifted off their roller bearing mountings. In addition, the aircraft catapult was put out of

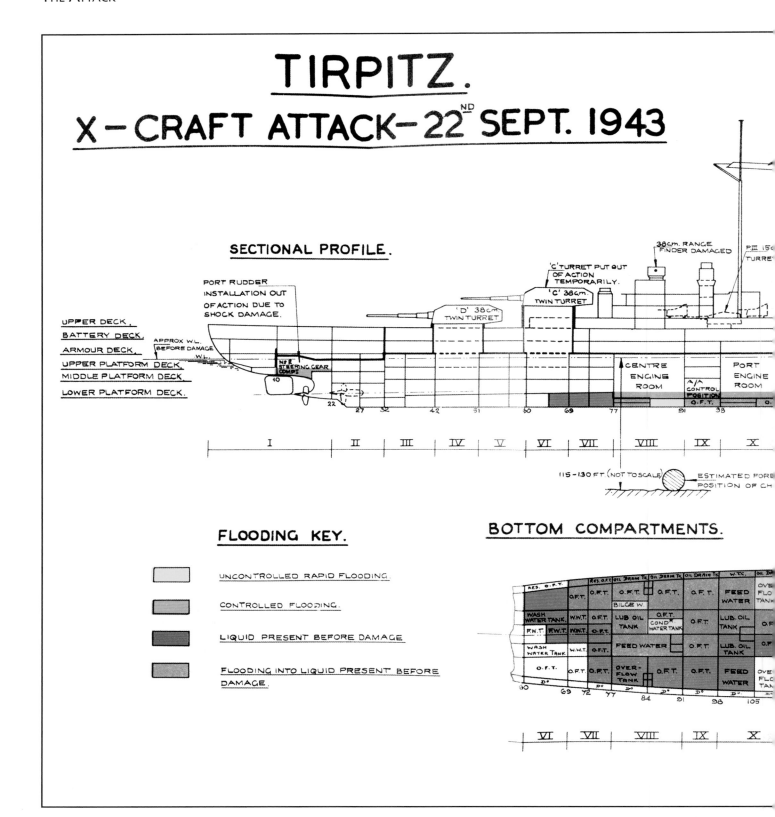

TIRPITZ.
X-CRAFT ATTACK-22ND SEPT. 1943

SECTIONAL PROFILE.

PORT RUDDER
INSTALLATION OUT
OF ACTION DUE TO
SHOCK DAMAGE.

'C' TURRET PUT OUT
OF ACTION
TEMPORARILY.

'C' 38cm.
TWIN TURRET

'D' 38cm.
TWIN TURRET

38cm. RANGE
FINDER DAMAGED

P.III 150
TURRE

UPPER DECK.
BATTERY DECK.
ARMOUR DECK.
UPPER PLATFORM DECK.
MIDDLE PLATFORM DECK.
LOWER PLATFORM DECK.

APPROX W.L.
BEFORE DAMAGE
W.L.

N° 2
STEERING GEAR
COMP.

CENTRE
ENGINE
ROOM

A/A
CONTROL
POSITION

PORT
ENGINE
ROOM

Q.F.T.

I   II   III   IV   V   VI   VII   VIII   IX   X

115-130 FT (NOT TO SCALE)   ESTIMATED FORE
POSITION OF CH

FLOODING KEY.

UNCONTROLLED RAPID FLOODING.

CONTROLLED FLOODING.

LIQUID PRESENT BEFORE DAMAGE

FLOODING INTO LIQUID PRESENT BEFORE
DAMAGE.

BOTTOM COMPARTMENTS.

VI   VII   VIII   IX   X

action, three of four flak directors were damaged and nearly all optical rangefinders were found to be defective. Surprisingly, 13 years after the war, German Admiral Karl Doenitz wrote that only one midget submarine had penetrated the *Tirpitz'* defences.

Clearly, Churchill's 'Beast' was not going anywhere for a long time, though it took the Admiralty some time to learn just how effective the X-craft raid had been. Interrogated at the German Admiralty at Eckernförde, Schleswig-Holstein, northern Germany on 17 May and 8 June 1945,

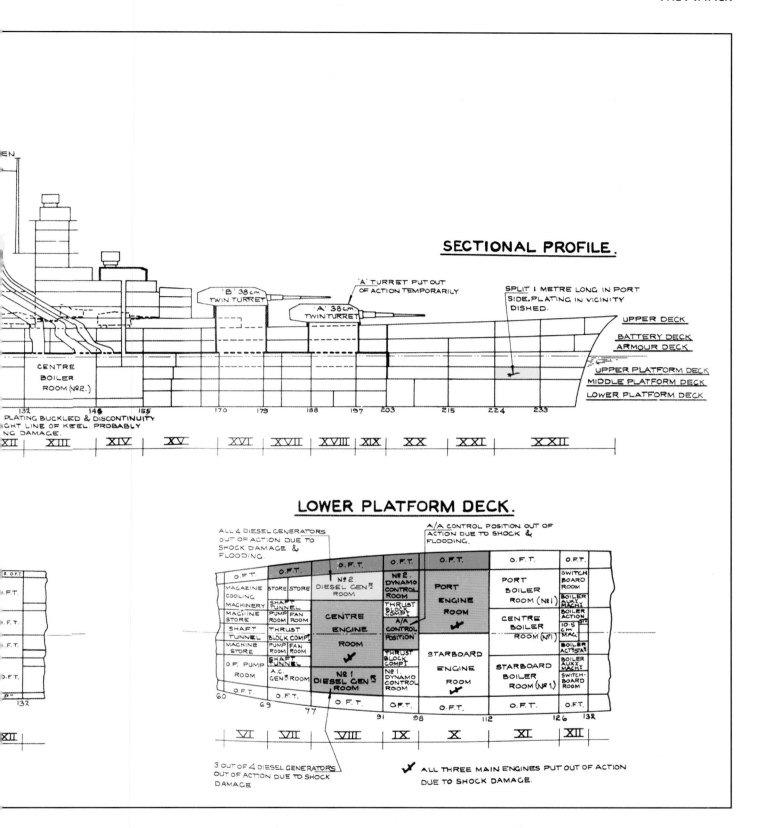

SECTIONAL PROFILE.

'B' 38cm TWIN TURRET

'A' TURRET PUT OUT OF ACTION TEMPORARILY

'A' 38cm TWIN TURRET

SPLIT I METRE LONG IN PORT SIDE. PLATING IN VICINITY DISHED.

CENTRE BOILER ROOM (Nº2.)

PLATING BUCKLED & DISCONTINUITY
GHT LINE OF KEEL. PROBABLY
NG DAMAGE.

UPPER DECK
BATTERY DECK
ARMOUR DECK
UPPER PLATFORM DECK
MIDDLE PLATFORM DECK
LOWER PLATFORM DECK

LOWER PLATFORM DECK.

ALL 4 DIESEL GENERATORS OUT OF ACTION DUE TO SHOCK DAMAGE & FLOODING.

A/A CONTROL POSITION OUT OF ACTION DUE TO SHOCK & FLOODING.

3 OUT OF 4 DIESEL GENERATORS OUT OF ACTION DUE TO SHOCK DAMAGE

✔ ALL THREE MAIN ENGINES PUT OUT OF ACTION DUE TO SHOCK DAMAGE.

Fregatten-Kapitän (Ing.) Eichler was engineer officer of the *Tirpitz* between June 1942 and October 1944 and was the best qualified to give the account of just how badly the *Tirpitz* had been damaged.

He told his interrogators 'the shafts could not be turned. The diesel generators in the flooded compartments were also severely damaged by shock', and, in confirming the detail already established by the Royal Navy added: 'The repairs were commenced in October, 1943, and finished in March, 1944, just before the Fleet Air Arm bombing attack'.

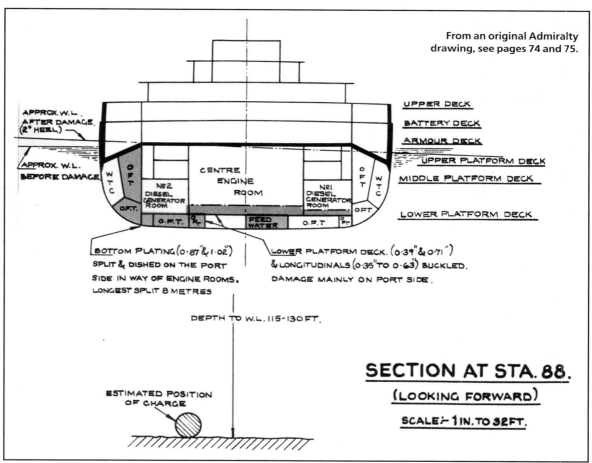

Above: Tirpitz listing to port after the X-craft attack. *(JA)*

Left: The day after the attack on *Tirpitz* aerial reconnaissance, by RAF Spitfires, shows the ship immobilised behind the anti-torpedo nets surrounded by leaking oil. The area of oil stretched for approximately 2 miles (3.2km). *(IWM)*

From an original Admiralty drawing, see pages 74 and 75.

APPROX. W.L. AFTER DAMAGE. (2° HEEL.)

APPROX. W.L. BEFORE DAMAGE.

UPPER DECK

BATTERY DECK

ARMOUR DECK

UPPER PLATFORM DECK

MIDDLE PLATFORM DECK

LOWER PLATFORM DECK

CENTRE ENGINE ROOM

No2 DIESEL GENERATOR ROOM

No1 DIESEL GENERATOR ROOM

WTC OFT OFT. O.F.T. FEED WATER O.F.T OFT WTC

BOTTOM PLATING (0·87" & 1·02") SPLIT & DISHED ON THE PORT SIDE IN WAY OF ENGINE ROOMS. LONGEST SPLIT 8 METRES

LOWER PLATFORM DECK. (0·39" & 0·71") & LONGITUDINALS (0·35" TO 0·63") BUCKLED. DAMAGE MAINLY ON PORT SIDE.

DEPTH TO W.L. 115-130 FT.

ESTIMATED POSITION OF CHARGE

SECTION AT STA. 88.

(LOOKING FORWARD)

SCALE :- 1 IN. TO 32 FT.

APPENDIX A - DETAILED ACCOUNTS OF DAMAGE

A.1 - DAMAGE SUSTAINED AS A RESULT OF "X" - CRAFT ATTACK IN KAA FJORD,
22nd SEPTEMBER, 1943 ("OPERATION SOURCE")

1.1 Narrative and Evidence

See Section III.3 of this Volume and Section 6 of Volume 2.

1.2 Weapons used

Each midget submarine ('X' craft) used in the attack carried two detachable side charges, resembling in shape the main tanks of a normal submarine, each of which contained two tons of Amatex. The charges were fitted with clock time fuzes which could be set before release. Four such charges from two X-craft were released under TIRPITZ, one under the port side of Section VIII (centre engine room), one abreast port side of the fore end of the ship and two close to one another abreast the port side of 'B' turret and rather further from the ship. These charges were off the port side of the ship after the fore end had been moved to starboard as a precautionary measure. Two of these four charges, namely the one under the engine room and one off the port bow, are known to have detonated within a fraction of a second of each other.

1.3 The Depth of Water

3.1 The depth of water in the anchorage varied between 35 and 40 metres (i.e. approximately between 115 and 130 feet) and the ship's draught at the time was about 10 metres (about 33 feet).

1.4 Subsequent Events

4.1 The two heavy explosions occurred at about 0812 G.M.T. and caused heavy spray but no appreciable water columns. The whole ship was shaken voilently. All lights and most of the electrical equipment failed immediately. The mooring cables remained intact and the ship listed gradually 2 degrees to port.

1.5 Structural Damage (See Figure A.1)

5.1 The bottom plating in way of the engine rooms was split and dished, the longest split being about 8 metres (approximately 26 feet). The inner bottom and longitudinals in the damaged area were forced upwards and buckled and all the pipes, including condenser inlets and outlets, were subjected to shock.

5.2 At the fore end the explosion of the second charge caused a small split about 1 metre (3.3 feet) long in the port side plating of Section XXII between the upper and middle platform decks. Plating in the vicinity was dished.

5.3 Whipping of the whole ship was most probably responsible for a sudden discontinuity in the straight line of keel and buckled panels of bottom plating in Section XI of the ship. (See Section 4.5 of Appendix B).

1.6 Flooding

6.1 Double bottom compartments in Sections VII to X (mainly on the port side) and No.2 diesel generator room were flooded, and leakage into the port and centre engine rooms, No.1 diesel-generator room, No.2 dynamo control room, the after anti-aircraft control position and No.2 steering gear compartment, was controlled by pumping. This flooding caused TIRPITZ to heel to port 2 degrees. It was estimated that 800 tons of water entered the ship.

6.2 All pumps were put out of action by lack of electric power but one hour after the explosion the centre and port engine rooms were pumped out and, by 1800, No.2 diesel-generator room had been pumped out using the hull and fire pumps.

A.1 - DAMAGE SUSTAINED AS A RESULT OF "OPERATION SOURCE" (Contd.)

1.7 Damage to machinery

All turbine feet, plummer-blocks, thrust blocks and much of the auxiliary machinery were distorted or cracked and as a result the propeller shafts could not be turned. The main defects were in Sections VII to IX. Damage to the port unit was more intense, for example, the port condenser and turbine casings were fractured. None of the boilers could be flashed up for some time because the auxiliary burners were damaged, particularly in the after boiler room; failure of electric current also prevented the fitted pumps being started. The damage took six months to repair.

1.8 Damage to Armament

All turrets jumped off their roller paths and turret clips were stretched. 'A' and 'C' turrets were put out of action temporarily and P.III 15 cm. twin turret was jammed. The after anti-aircraft control position was put out of action by shock and flooding and a considerable amount of range-finding and other optical equipment were severely damaged and needed replacement, including the equipment in the 38 cm. director control towers and the 15 cm. secondary armament control towers on either side of the bridge.

1.9 Damage to Electrical Equipment

Most of the ship's lighting and nearly all her electrical equipment, including her W/T equipment, were put out of action by the explosions. There was some delay before a diesel generator and a small auxiliary plant could be started to supply the ship with power. Turbo-generators were brought into operation about $2\frac{1}{2}$ hours after the explosions. Seven of the eight diesel-generators were put out of action by shock damage to casings and cracked holding-down bolts.

1.10 Damage to Communications Equipment

In addition to the temporary failure of communications and W/T equipment generally, due to loss of power, much of the W/T equipment and aerials were permanently damaged. Similar breakdowns occurred in the radar and echo ranging equipment.

1.11 Miscellaneous Damage

The port rudder installation was put out of action by shock which caused the stuffing gland to leak and the steering gear compartment to flood. Fire and bilge pumps were put out of action by electrical failures and mechanical damage. Two aircraft were badly damaged.

Original Admiralty documents.

Such was the success of the
X-craft in many attacks that they
must be seen as the most cost-
effective submarines ever built.

5

THE CREWS

The honours spread among a few men were considerable and, like the casualties, seemingly out of proportion to the numbers involved. Yet there can be no denying the courage of those involved. Lieutenants Cameron and Place were both awarded the highest honour, the Victoria Cross (VC). There were Distinguished Service Orders (DSOs) for Sub Lieutenants Aitken, Kendall and Lorimer. ERA 4 Goddard received a Conspicuous Gallantry Medal (CGM). Lieutenant Hudspeth was awarded the Distinguished Service Cross (DSC) following his skill, coolness and leadership in surmounting all sorts of disappointments and frustrations. Others received a Mention in Despatches - among them Lieutenant Henty-Creer whose relatives fought for years in an effort to see that he, too, should receive the VC. The operational crews who did not get chance to take part in the attack because of the losses of *X8* and *X9* were to get their opportunities in successful midget submarine operations in Europe and South East Asia. *Tirpitz* was not sunk, much to the chagrin of the men who laid charges under or near the battleship. After the

Left: **Engine Room Artificer 4th Class (ERA4) E. Goddard from *X6*. For his part in the attack he was awarded the Conspicuous Gallantry Medal (CGM).** *(AN)*

Far left: **Sub Lieutenant Robert Aitken, RN part of the attack crew in *X7*. He was awarded the Distinguished Service Order (DSO).** *(AN)*

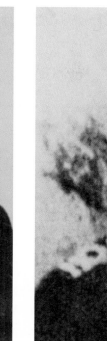

Right: **Sub Lieutenant R.H. Kendall, RNVR, part of the attack crew of** *X6.* **He was awarded the Distinguished Service Order (DSO).** *(AN)*

Far right: **Lieutenant Donald Cameron, RN Commanding Officer of** *X6.* **He was awarded the Victoria Cross and was considered to be the best navigator in the raid on** *Tirpitz.* **After the war Cameron continued in the Royal Navy serving with the submarine service until his death on 10 April 1962 at the age of 45. He had achieved the rank of Commander.** *(AN)*

Right: **Lieutenant Basil Charles Godfrey Place, RN Commanding Officer of** *X7* **was awarded the Victoria Cross. Place later retrained to become a Fleet Air Arm pilot eventually serving with No 801 squadron on board HMS** *Glory* **in the Korean War.** *(UK)*

attack, *Tirpitz* was really reduced in status from being a constant threat to convoy operations to that of a nuisance. Thousands of German workers were brought to northern Norway to work on repairing the damage caused. In December 1943 there was more good news for the Royal Navy when *Scharnhorst*, attempting to attack convoys, was intercepted by the battleship HMS *Duke of York* leading a powerful supporting group of cruisers and destroyers - and it was the cruiser HMS *Jamaica* that finished a battered *Scharnhorst* with a torpedo. This also pleased Winston Churchill, who

wrote in Volume 5 of *The Second World War*: 'Although the fate of the crippled *Tirpitz* was delayed for nearly a year, the sinking of the *Scharnhorst* not only removed the worst menace to our Arctic convoys, but gave new freedom to our Home Fleet.

'We no longer had to be prepared at our average moment against German heavy ships breaking out into the Atlantic at their selected moment. This was an important relief.' As this is being written in the build up to the 60th anniversary of Victory in Europe celebrations 1945, this is one good reason (along with the 60th anniversary in 2003 of the raid itself) why there is continuing interest in the feats of the midget submarine crews. Continuing, rather than renewed, for the triumph of these men has never ceased to stir people interested in the history of World War Two. One question remains - just what did happen to *X5*? Three reports by Admiral (Submarines) were sent to the Admiralty on Operation 'Source' and were published in the *London Gazette* - having been declassified - on 10 February 1948.

BR 1736 (22) A is a two-volume account of all attacks carried out by British forces on the *Tirpitz* and can be seen in The National Archives (Public Record Office) as ADM 234/349. The Battle Summary No.29

Left: **The attack and passage crews of *X5*. Back row, L to R: Lt. J. V. Terry-Lloyd, SANF, S/Lt. D. Malcolm, RNVR, Lt. H. Henty-Creer, RNVR, S/Lt. T. J. Nelson, RNVR,. Front row, L to R: Acting Leading Seaman Element, Stoker 1st class Garrity and ERA Mortiboys.** *(RNSM)*

Left: **The attack and passage crews of *X6*. Back row from left (L) to right (R): S/Lt. J. T. Lorimer, RNVR, Lt. D. Cameron, RNR, Lt. A. Wilson, RNVR, Front row L to R: Stoker 1st class Oakley, unidentified, S/Lt. Kendall, RNVR, and ERA4 E. Goddard.** *(RNSM)*

Right: **The attack and passage crews for *X7*. Back row, L to R: S/Lt. R. Aitken RNVR, S/Lt. L. Whittam, RNVR, Lt. B. C.G. Place DSC, RN, Lt. P. H. Philip SANF(V). Front row, L to R: Leading Seaman J. J. Magennis, Stoker 1st class Luck and ERA4 Whitley.** *(RNSM)*

states the part played by *X5* is not known, as mentioned above. Yet a footnote on the same page claimed that Rear-Admiral Submarines 'remarked that it was clear from the position in which *X5* was found that Lieutenant Henty-Creer and his crew showed courage of the highest order in penetrating the fleet anchorage and that they lived up to the highest traditions of the service'. Bearing in mind the time between that report and publication of the combined reports in 1948, the final report had the benefit of results from debriefing the returning prisoners of war and learning more from their accounts.

According to the official report, *X5* was sunk at 0843. A third midget submarine had been seen by German crewmen (and at least two of the X-craft survivors, now prisoners-of-war), approximately 500yds (457m) beyond *Tirpitz* and the net protection. The gunners on *Tirpitz* opened fire and claimed to have hit and sunk this craft, and the area was also depth charged by the destroyer Z-27. Interestingly, though wreckage of *X7* was recovered by the Germans, no trace was found

of *X5* or the crew. It was considered *X5* had been completely destroyed by the explosions. In 1988, Lt. Henty-Creer's sister Pamela and Australian writer Frank Walker published *The Mystery of X5* after long and determined efforts to prove that *X5* had laid a charge by *Tirpitz* and may have been making an escape when spotted. In 1973 and 1976 members of the British Sub Aqua Club mounted diving expeditions in Kaafjord (now Kafjord) in an effort to help to solve the mystery. Leader of the expedition Peter Cornish declared there was no trace of *X5* or crew in the fjord. Despite the understandable anguish, determination and travails of Henty-Creer's mother Eulalie, his sisters Deirdre, Pamela and her British Army officer husband Gerard Mellor, Henty-Creer was not awarded a VC, though he was originally recommended for the medal.

Pamela Mellor and Frank Walker raised some interesting, and some plausible theories. They questioned the Royal Navy for failing to investigate the matter thoroughly, in their view. The two officers who did receive the VC had their feats witnessed by fellow officers. So

Left: **The attack and passage crews for** *X8.* **Back row, L to R: Lt. Marsden, RANVR, Lt. L. B. McFarlane, RAN, Lt. J.E. Smart, RNVR S/Lt. R. Hindmarsh, RN.. Front row, L to R: ERA4 J. Murray, Stoker 1st class Robinson, Leading Seaman H. A. Pomeroy.** *(RNSM)*

there was no need to use the thirteenth of the Victoria Cross rules and ordinances - which in essence say officers can elect one of their own, and the other ranks or ratings one of their own, to receive a VC if senior officers are not there to witness spectacular acts of bravery. There was insufficient proof for awarding one to the CO of *X5*. A further complication for the Henty-Creer relatives was that in 1946 governments of the British dominions involved (now Commonwealth nations) had agreed no further World War Two awards or decorations would be made.

At the time of writing there are three living survivors of the attack on *Tirpitz* - Robert Aitken and John Lorimer in the United Kingdom and the diver of *X6*, 'Dickie' Kendall in Canada. Others, part of Operation 'Source' if not the attack itself, also survive. Robert Aitken viewed the Germans' treatment of him as a prisoner as 'correct' and agreed on return to freedom and home to take part in a 'shoot the line' (publicity) tour to remind younger men that there was still a war on against the Japanese. He was promised a visit to the United States of America – 'but then came VJ Day and America was off.' He also spent a few months

duty on the Kiel Canal in Germany before leaving the Royal Navy to return to his chosen profession of accountancy. John Lorimer retired as a lieutenant-commander in 1960 and is a forestry consultant.

Vernon Coles also left the Royal Navy in 1960 as a chief engine room artificer. He was involved in further midget submarine operations with fellow frustrated *X9* operational officer, Australian Lt. Max Shean. In the later craft, *X24*, they went back to Norway to attack a floating dock in Bergen, but sank the 7,500-ton *Barenfels* ammunition ship instead.

Even so, it was a highly successful operation. Shean received the DSO and Coles was awarded the Distinguished Service Medal (DSM). *X24* was used again in September with a different crew who succeeded in severely damaging the floating dock. For their part in an underwater cable-cutting operation off Saigon in 1945, Shean received a bar to his DSO and Coles was awarded a Mention in Despatches. 'Max Shean and I were the longest serving operationally. We were the only two to sail on three attacks', Coles told the author. Shean's fellow Australian Lt. Hudspeth (*X10*)

was awarded two bars to his DSC when serving on *X20*, first in reconnoitring the D-Day beaches in Normandy, then acting as 'marker' for the incoming invasion force landing craft. And two more Australians, Lieutenants B. M. McFarlane and W.J. Marsden, disappointed when the loss of *X8* prevented their joining in the *Tirpitz* assault, lost their lives when *X22* was sunk on exercise in the Pentland Firth, north Scotland in 1944. Sub. Lt. Bruce Enzer, of Hudspeth's *X10* crew, died in a diving accident from *XE3* in July 1945, having been promoted to lieutenant.

As has already been mentioned, 'Mick' Magennis (*X7* passage crew) earned the VC when, as Acting Leading Seaman James Joseph Magennis, from *XE3* and in very tight circumstances, he attached limpet mines to the Japanese cruiser *Takao*, near Singapore. Though exhausted, he left *XE3* again to clear a limpet that was dangerously close to the midget submarine. Magennis died aged 66 on 11 February 1986 in Halifax, Yorkshire and was cremated at nearby Shipley.

The two VCs of the *Tirpitz* raid both remained in the Royal Navy. Donald Cameron, regarded by fellow X-craft men as the best navigator of all, had tried to join the RAF but was rejected because he was under-age. So, having joined the RN, he served in an armed merchant cruiser before volunteering for submarines, serving on HM Submarine *Sturgeon*. Then he joined the X-craft and was in at the start of *X3's* trials and tribulations through to the incredible *X6* events of 22 September 1943. He reached the rank of commander and died aged 45 on 10 April 1961 - at Haslar, not far from HMS *Dolphin*. He was cremated at Portchester, Hampshire and his ashes were scattered from HM Submarine *Thule* off the Nab Tower in the Solent. His name is commemorated in Cameron Close, Gosport.

Basil Charles Godfrey Place added to his VC and DSC by being appointed Companion, Order of the Bath (CB); and Commander, Royal Victorian Order (CVO) 1991. He added to his skills beneath the waves by becoming a Fleet Air Arm pilot. As a commander, he added to his combat experience with No. 801 Squadron flying from the Light Fleet Carrier HMS *Glory* in the Korean War, 1952 to 1953. Among many appointments before he retired as a

Left: The attack and passage crews for *X10*. Back row, L to R: S/Lt. G. Harding, RNVR, Lt. K. R. Hudspeth, RANVR, S/Lt. B. Enzer, RNVR, S/Lt. E. V. Page, RNVR. Front row, L to R: ERA4 H. J. Fisherleigh, Acting PO Brookes, ERA4 Tillley. *(RNSM)*

rear-admiral was Deputy Director of Air Warfare, 1960 to 1962. Place died aged 73 in Holborn, London on 27 December 1994. He is buried in the churchyard of Corton Denham, near Sherborne, Dorset. Apart from his headstone in Dorset he has portraits hanging in RNSS *Mackenzie* and HMS *Dolphin* and his medals are in the IWM.

As mentioned above X-craft continued to serve well after the attack on *Tirpitz*. Sadly, none of the six used in Operation 'Source' remains intact - although the bow of *X7* can be viewed at the Imperial War Museum's Duxford site, along with the complete *X51*. A direct development from early X-craft, she was named HMS *Stickleback*, built by Vickers Armstrong Limited at Barrow-in-Furness, launched in 1954 and served until 1957. She was sold in 1965 to the Royal Swedish Navy (RSN) named *Spiggen* (*Stickleback*) and used mainly for training. The RSN presented *X51* to the Imperial War Museum and the Royal Navy brought her home in 1976. A section of both sides has been cut out and glazed over so visitors to Hangar 3 at Duxford can walk through and view the engine space. One wartime X-craft can still be seen at the Royal Navy Submarine Museum in Gosport - *X24* of Bergen fame. So can a net cutter, powered by hydraulic pressure -

provided from the boat through pipes with a combination of water and compressed air - and which a diver could use with one hand, a considerable advantage. The company Starkie Gardner, makers of the then standard navy-pattern cutters, produced the improved Mark VI.

The Royal Navy ceased to use midget submarines in 1958, though since then there has been evidence of similar vessels being used by the former Soviet Navy, Iran and North Korea. With the increasing accent on expeditionary and littoral warfare by certain Western navies, particularly the Americans and British, can midget submarines make a comeback? It is unlikely for most navies, because planners for tomorrow's warfare are concentrating on unmanned vehicles for sea, land and air operations.

Perhaps the last word should be left with former X-craft commander, historian and former Director of the Royal Navy Submarine Museum, Richard Compton-Hall. In his book *Submarine Warfare* he wrote that the invaluable operations of X-craft 'were accomplished at remarkably little cost in terms of either men or material. The expression had not been coined in World War Two, but X-craft must have been the most "cost-effective" submarines ever built'.

Right: **X24**
(**Exultant**)
approaching
moorings. The
mooring cable is
clearly visible
attached to a ring
on the bow of the
vessel. This is the
X-craft which was
used on the two
successful raids at
Bergen in 1944.
(RNSM)

From the time the Tirpitz was launched at Wilhelmshaven 22 air attacks were made against the ship by the Royal Air Force and the Fleet Air Arm.

AIR ATTACKS

When in April 1944 there were signs that the *Tirpitz* had been repaired sufficiently to move for refit to a Baltic port, aircraft from the carriers HMS *Victorious* and *Furious* attacked her with heavy bombs, and she was once more immobilised. This attack on 3 April 1944 was mounted from six aircraft carriers: HM Ships *Emperor, Fencer, Furious, Pursuer, Searcher* and *Victorious*. The Fleet Air Arm Squadrons, with aircraft types, were: Nos. 800 and 804 (Hellcat), No. 842 (Wildcat), Nos. 827, 829, 830 and 831 (Barracuda), Nos. 801 and 887 (Seafire), Nos. 881, 882, 896 and 898 (Wildcat), and also Nos. 1834 and 1836 (Corsair). Four cruisers and fourteen destroyers led by the battleship HMS *Anson*, supported the carriers. Twenty-one Fairey Barracuda dive bombers protected by 40 fighters were to hit the target ship in two strikes. One Barracuda was lost in each strike and just one fighter. *Tirpitz* was struck with 10 x 500lb (227kg) and four 1,600lb (726kg) bombs, suffered over 400 casualties and was put out of action for a further

Left: **10.5cm Flak (anti-aircraft) guns on the upper deck of *Tirpitz*. During both raids on 3 April 1944 these guns fired 506 rounds at the attacking aircraft. The vessel is en-route to Bogen, Norway after the abandonment of Operation 'Sportpalast', 9 March, 1942.** *(JA)*

Right: **After the series of attacks by the Fleet Air Arm,** *Tirpitz* **was moved to Alten Fjord (Tromsö) for repairs.** *(IWM)*

Below: **Repairs almost complete after the attack by X-craft.** *(IWM)*

three months. The Royal Air Force (RAF) now took up the attack from a base in North Russia, and succeeded in causing further damage, which led to the *Tirpitz* being removed to Trømso Fjord, which was 200 miles (322km) nearer to Britain and within the extreme range of home-based RAF heavy bombers. The Germans had now abandoned hope of getting the ship home for repair and had written her off as a seagoing fighting unit. On November 12, twenty-nine specially fitted Lancasters of No.5 Group Bomber Command RAF, including those of No. 617 Squadron, famous for the Mohne and Eder dam raids, struck the decisive blow, with 12,000lb (5,443 kg) 'Tallboy' bombs. The crews had to fly over 2,000 miles (3,219km) from their bases in Scotland, but the weather was clear and three bombs hit the target. The *Tirpitz* capsized at her moorings, more than half of her crew of 1,900 men being killed, at the cost of one bomber, whose crew survived.

'All British heavy ships were now free to move to the Far East', stated Churchill.

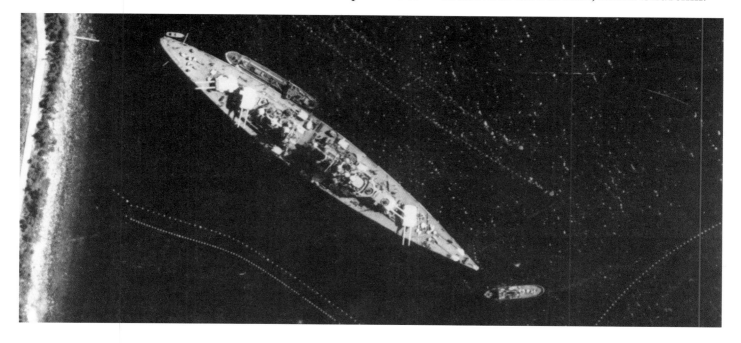

Above: **Barracuda pilots being briefed for the raid on *Tirpitz* in Kaafjord.** *(IWM)*

Left: **A Grumman Hellcat, the first aircraft in the fighter escort, begins the take-off run from the deck of HMS *Emperor*. Each of the two strikes in Operation 'Tungsten', 3 April 1944, was escorted by 20 Grumman Wildcats, 10 Hellcats and 10 Vought Corsairs.** *(IWM)*

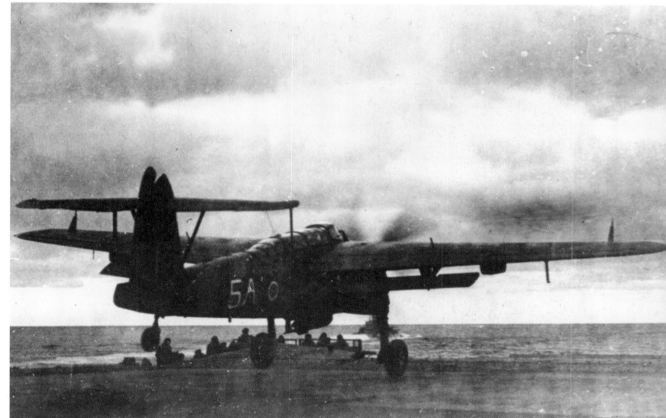

Above: **Smoke generators are ignited to cover the target area before the Fleet Air Arm dive-bombing raid.** *(IWM)*

Right: **A Fairey Barracuda leaves the flight deck of HMS *Victorious* to attack *Tirpitz* in Operation 'Tungsten'.** *(IWM)*

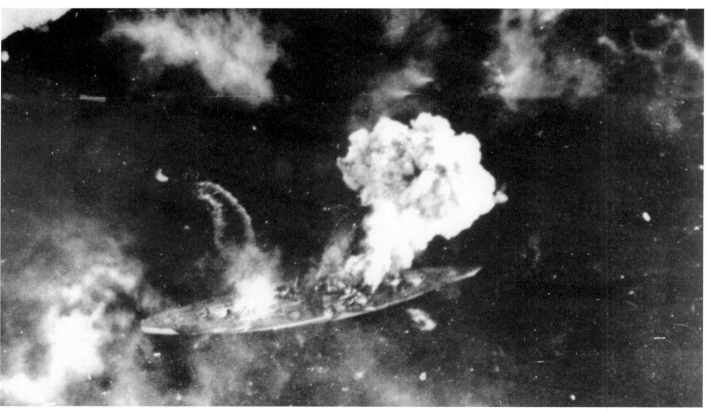

Left: **A 500lb (227Kg) bomb explodes close to the bridge on** *Tirpitz.* **At the top of the photograph a Fairey Barracuda banks away after the attack, note the shadow of the aircraft on the side of the mountain.** *(IWM)*

Below: **The smoke clears from the bridge area. The white specks on both photographs are anti-aircraft shells bursting.** *(IWM)*

Right: **A Barracuda about to land after the raid on *Tirpitz*. Although an ungainly-looking aircraft it was a very effective dive-bomber. (IWM)**

Below: **Three Fairy Barracudas return from the second strike in Operation 'Tungsten', 3 April 1944, photographed from the deck of HMS *Emperor*. The carrier in the background is HMS *Victorious*. (IWM)**

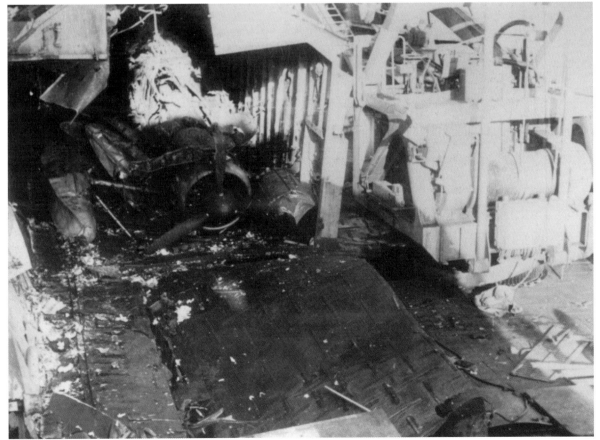

Above: **Flight deck crews rush to clear the aircraft forward ready for the next to land. The first strike was carried out by 21 Barracudas of No 827 and No 830 squadrons of No 8 TBR wing. The second strike was by 19 Barracudas of No 829 and No 831 squadrons of No 52 TBR wing.** *(IWM)*

Left: **One of the two Arado Ar196 aircraft carried on *Tirpitz* was destroyed in its hangar. These float-equipped aircraft were launched by steam catapult and used for reconnaissance.** *(JA)*

Above: **Bomb damage was limited to very heavy splinter damage to the upper deck, flak guns and communications equipment.** *(JA)*

Right: **Heavy splinter damage caused by an instantaneous-fused 500lb (227Kg) bomb. In the raid on 3 April 1944, casualty numbers were 122 crew members on *Tirpitz* killed whilst 316 were wounded.** *(JA)*

Left: **A 12,000lb Tallboy bomb hits *Tirpitz* during Operation 'Catechism' on 12 November 1944. This is one of three raids carried out with Avro Lancasters of the RAF. The other raids were 'Paravane', 15 September 1944, and 'Obviate', 29 October 1944. Close examination of the photograph shows waves at the stern where the vessel has 'bounced' under the impact of the bomb.** *(IWM)*

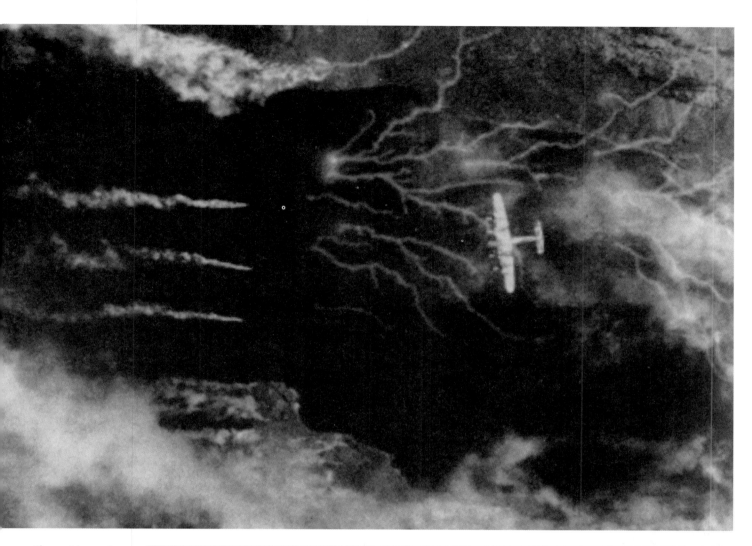

Above: **A Lancaster approaches the target through tracer fire. Smoke floats have been ignited in an effort to conceal the target.** *(JA)*

Right: **This is thought to be the Tallboy exploding which finished** *Tirpitz.* **Another bomb has exploded on the shore, leaving a massive crater which remains to this day.** *(IWM)*

Above: **On 12 November 1944** *Tirpitz* **was struck by two Tallboy bombs and a near miss to port which caused severe flooding and listing. A massive detonation followed as X magazine exploded and the ship capsized.** *(IWM)*

Left: **The remains of** *X7* **as found in Kaafjord with** *X51 Stickleback* **as a backdrop in the Imperial War Museum, Duxford, Cambs.** *(PH)*

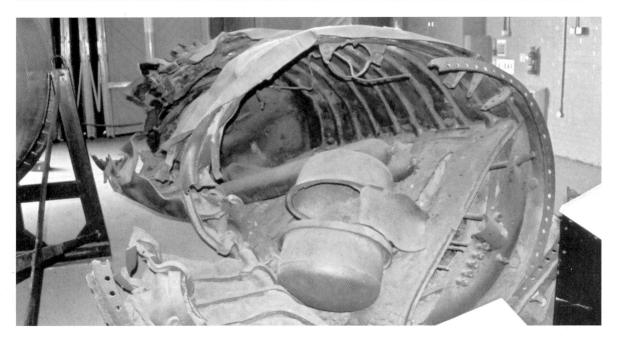